D0776751

Agenda for Theology

By THOMAS C. ODEN

After Therapy What?
Agenda for Theology
Game Free
The Intensive Group Experience
Kerygma and Counseling
Radical Obedience: The Ethics of Rudolf Bultmann
Should Treatment Be Terminated?
TAG: Transactional Awareness Game

Agenda for Theology

THOMAS C. ODEN

Published in San Francisco by Harper & Row, Publishers
New York, Hagerstown, San Francisco, London

Biblical quotations, unless otherwise noted, are from *The New English Bible*, © the Delegates of the Oxford University Press and the Syndics of the Cambridge University Press 1961, 1970. Reprinted by permission.

For information, address Harper & Row, Publishers, Inc., 10 East 53rd Street, New York, NY 10022. Published simultaneously in Canada by Fitzhenry & Whiteside Limited, Toronto.

FIRST EDITION

Designed by Jim Mennick

Library of Congress Cataloging in Publication Data

Oden, Thomas C

AGENDA FOR THEOLOGY.

1. Theology—20th century. I. Title.
BT28.033 230 78-19506
ISBN 0-06-066347-2

79 80 81 82 83 10 9 8 7 6 5 4 3 2 1

For Albert Cook Outler,
my first and finest theological teacher

Contents

Preface

WHAT'S happening in theology today? It is a little like a pregnancy around the fourth month. A quiet, complex, inconspicuous formation is taking place, but its detailed features are not yet visible. The moment of birth is not yet near, but the developing embryo is already alive and kicking. Viewed from a distance, the growth is slow and hardly discernible. To many it may seem as though nothing at all is happening. Viewed from within, however, there is spectacular growth, complex formation, rising strength, growing readiness, emergent consciousness, and vast possibility.

At whom is this agenda aimed? Mainly at the pastor involved daily in the care of souls but secondarily at theological professionals, religious leaders, and laypersons who have reason to be fascinated or disturbed by the ups and downs of theology in our time. It may be viewed as a minority report to the steering committee. The majority report is already in: Keep on trying to accommodate to modernity, do not rest until you find credentials of acceptability, and barter off whatever you can to get the proffered blessing of modern psychologists, power brokers, and pacesetters. The minority report says, It is just this accommodation that has brought us to the brink of disaster, identity confusion, and the worst case of Christian amnesia that the church has had for a long time. It is a time to remember well, ask tough questions, and, above all, not sell our birthright for a mess of pottage.

Two brief working definitions, to be developed further in Chapter 2, will help the reader move quickly into the argument. I use *classical Christianity* to refer to the ancient ecumenical consensus of Christianity's first millennium, particularly as expressed in scripture and in the Seven Ecumenical Councils affirmed by Catholic, Protestant, and Orthodox traditions. By *modernity* I mean the overarching ideology of the modern period, characterized as it is by autonomous individualism, secularization, naturalistic reductionism, and narcissistic hedonism, which assumes that recent modes of knowing the truth are vastly superior to all older ways—a view that has recently presided over the precipitous deterioration of social structures and processes in the third quarter of the twentieth century. My aim is to help free persons from feeling intimidated by modernity, which, while it often seems awesome, is rapidly losing its moral power, and to grasp the emerging vision of a postmodern Christian orthodoxy.

Although none of the following persons should be held responsible for exaggerations in my argument, I wish to express sincere gratitude to the Drew University colleagues who provided helpful critical responses to all or parts of this manuscript: to Paul Hardin (university president), John Ollam (physics), James M. O'Kane (sociology), Johannes Morsinck (philosophy), Neal Riemer (political philosophy), Roger Wescott and Leedom Lefferts (anthropology), Philip Jensen (psychology); to colleagues in theological and religious studies, Bard Thompson, James E. Kirby, Stanley Menking, Russell Richey, Michael Ryan, David Graybeal, Charles Rice, Neill Hamilton, Darrell Doughty, Donald G. Jones, William Stroker, Shirley Sugerman, and William Presnell; to Joan Engelsman of the Women's Resource Center; as well as to graduate students Dulcie Gannett, Larry Bowden, and Janet Gnall, and to Joseph Imbriaco. To three friends in ministry whose personal warmth and insight have deeply affected my views I am especially grateful: Jackson Smith, James Hampson, and Frank Mabee.

The depth of my vexation over the naiveté of the value assumptions of the modern, massive, secular university situation will become evident in what follows. Those who recognize how deep this theme runs in my thinking will understand how grateful I am to be a part of an unusual, small, and excellent university with such superb colleagues.

T.C.O.

Drew Forest
Madison, New Jersey

Introduction: What Is Theology Coming To?

A PLASTIC plumbing-fixtures tycoon inherited from his Slavic uncle a baroque, antique, jeweled diadem of spectacular beauty and considerable historical importance. He had been entrusted to take care of it but knew nothing of its actual value and did not lift a finger to protect it. He considered it "just old junk." He hung it on an antelope horn on his mantel. Once in a while he enjoyed spinning it in the air, showing it off at employee parties, bending it, getting laughs. On certain occasions when he was in debt, he had been known to dig a jewel out and pawn it.

Isn't this much like the relation in which we moderns stand to classical Christianity? As moderns, we feel enormously superior to our Christian heritage. It is of little practical value to us, although we are still willing to keep it around. We would hardly feel good about throwing it away altogether, but it is little more to us than a mantel decoration or a souvenir of a trip long ago to Atlantic City.

The plastics magnate had received this diadem without any struggle or cost on his part, yet it had had great political significance to his immigrant uncle's family and nation. The magnate was unaware that there had been a time when many were willing to fight and die just to touch or behold the diadem. So it is that our perceptions of the value of something we are easily bequeathed without cost may be much more dim and vague than it is to those who have had to struggle desperately to win it or protect it.

Similarly, with Christianity, if we are to understand its original meaning or value we must come again to see it through the eyes of those who have had to struggle for it and maintain it. It is from the martyrs, saints, and prophets of Christian history, more than from recent riskless interpreters, that we learn of the value of classical Christianity. Without their instruction, Christianity becomes a mere recollection, a bored nodding of the head, the source of an occasional laugh, or, in emergency, an item to pawn.

The tycoon had a son who had always been curiously attracted to the diadem, wondered about it, and for some reason thought it was incomparably beautiful. When the son came of age, he made it his purpose to learn everything he could about the ornament. To his amazement, he found that for centuries it had been passed down from generation to generation as a revered symbol of the corporate identity, dignity, and freedom of a small, struggling group of patriots who had fought against great odds for their right to tend mountain vineyards in a small, far away land.

Just such a discovery is taking place in Christian awareness today. The sons and daughters of modernity are rediscovering the neglected beauty of classical Christian teaching. It is a moment of joy, of beholding anew what had been nearly forgotten, of hugging a lost child. This is the untold story of recent Christian thought. It is hard to see, because it is a search for roots, and roots are by definition underneath the surface. Popular media perceptions of religious events see only the surface, where apparently nothing is happening today in religious studies. But much is happening, deep below the quiet façade.

I have been astonished to discover that some of our best students, those who have grasped most deeply the hopes of modernity, fought for its political dreams, understood its psychological interpretations, appropriated its symbols, experienced its technological achievements and failures, its hedonic ecstasies and spiritual hungers—these keenest, most perceptive students are the ones most insistent on letting the ancient tradition speak for itself. They have had a bellyfull of the hyped claims of modern therapies and political messianism to make all things right. They are fascinated—and often passionately moved—by the primitive language of the apostolic tradition and the church fathers, undiluted by our contemporary efforts to soften it or make it easier or package it for smaller challenge but greater acceptability.

Finally my students got through to me. They do not want to hear a watered-down modern reinterpretation. They want nothing less than the substance of the faith of the apostles and martyrs without too much interference from those who doubt that they are tough enough to take it straight. They do not mind occasionally hearing my opinions, but they would far rather spend their valuable time listening directly to Paul's letter to Rome, to Irenaeus on heresy, to Cyprian on martyrdom, to the great ecumenical councils defining the heart of belief, to Anselm struggling to reason about God's existence, to Luther addressing the German nobility, or to Wesley writing his journal between long days on horseback.

This is what our students do not want to miss: a chance to experience the power of authentic Christian consciousness in the presence of a community of living faith, without heavy distortions by modern assumptions about what Christianity has recently been assumed to be. If we give them anything less, they experience a sense of dilution, a feeling that they have been cheated, that something crucial has been left out of their education. This cannot be explained simply as an afterburn of the Jesus movement, a recurrence of the charismatic impulse, a hunger for a past pietism, or a nostalgia for a more stable society (although all of these factors at times are influences). Rather, to our surprise, we are now meeting in our seminary classrooms the postmodern student who has already imbibed deeply of the best wellsprings of the finest modern universities and come away thirsty, who has gone through the long smorgasbord of pop psychologies and political ideologies and various alterations of consciousness by chemistry and by social experiment, and who now hungers for more nourishing food. This student may know well the rigor of the scientific laboratory but is quite clear that its results will not save his or her soul. We are dealing with a student who has been through the best the university has to offer and now is searching for a way of reconstruction, a way of return, a way of purgation.

These postmodern students have explored the edges and precipices of the ecstasies of modern freedom and have fallen into their share of its abysses. Having painfully experienced the limits of modernity, they are now engaging in a lengthy pilgrimage in which they have at long last stumbled, almost by accident, on the texts and spiritual directions and liturgies of classical Christianity. They have lived for twenty-plus years in a moral milieu in which that ancient and patristic Christian tradition has been put down, sentimentalized, or sugar-coated. But they know its deeper joy has hardly been touched.

This is what I mean by postmodern orthodoxy. Its spirit is embodied in the student who has been through the rigors of university education, often through the hazards of the drug scene, through the ups and downs of political engagement, through the head shrinks and group thinks of popular therapies, and through a dozen sexual messianisms, only to become weary of the pretentious motions of frenetic change. Finally they have come on Christ's living presence in the world in an actual community of Christians and now have set out to understand what has happened to them in the light of the classical texts of scripture and tradition.

Not all the postmodern orthodox are students. Some are driving cabs or growing cabbage or playing gigs or repairing BMW's or practicing law. It just happens that my personal vantage point for meeting them has been in a theological seminary, where they come to us on the rebound from profound disillusionments with modern trends and a hunger for spiritual roots.

This student generation in our seminaries is asking us far deeper questions than we are prepared to answer on the basis of the prevailing pop theologies of recent Protestantism. They can spot empty rhetoric a mile away. They will not abide our easy evasions or cheap reassurances. They want substance, not pablum. They may have their blind spots, but their hearing is perfect in the presence of double-talk. I know how penetrating their criticisms can be. I teach them daily. They expect us to deliver to them the available power of the

Christian heritage rather than trendy ideas of minor modern heretics.

These young people, the postmodern orthodox, both Jews and Christians, whose hopes and intuitions will be explored in what follows, are the unreported story of this decade of American religious consciousness. The popular press can see no reportable news here. But if one of these young people were to swallow a fish or crack someone on the head with a sign with a four-letter word on it or announce with gestures of importance that he or she had discovered a new coital position, you can bet that would be vigorously reported. But that is the nature of "news," and it is the very reason why religious teaching does well to pay less and less attention to the press's view of theological importance. When the media become fixated only on aberrations, especially those who imagine that they constitute some irrepressible wave of the future, they unconsciously collude with the encouragement of publicity for anyone who is odd, provocative, scandalous, or has his or her hat on backward. So this discussion is in part simply a report of what I am finding in the moral and intellectual appetites of the emerging generation of ministry, of how I am hoping to sharpen these conceptions and rectify misconceptions.

I

THE COURTSHIP OF MODERNITY

WHAT IS happening in theology today? Imagine a person who has been chronically sick, jaundiced, and immobilized by an unidentified virus. A powerful antibiotic has recently been introduced into the bloodstream. On the surface, it appears as though the patient is sick unto death, with no treatment known. But the potent healing force is hiddenly at work, successfully beginning to battle the infection day and night. The patient, however, remains miserable, and there is no obvious indication yet that a turning point has been reached.

I

In and Out of Season

FROM the point of view of social welfare, there are two types of theologians: employed and unemployed. In previous centuries, other important distinctions prevailed: semi-Pelagian / Augustinian, Unitarian / Trinitarian, Arian / Athanasian, Pedobaptist / Immersionist, Supralapsarian / Infralapsarian. Once upon a time these distinctions made all the difference. Life and death have hung on them. Now the most decisive distinction among theologians is not a theological distinction at all but an economic and sociological one: Are they working or not? The modern period in theology has abolished all these weary distinctions, and forged "significant new progress" by reducing all differences in theology to a single variable: Is the theologian employed? But even this distinction may be less significant than it sometimes seems to be.

One of our fondest objectives is to put unemployed theologians back to work. The problem is made more difficult by the fact that theology appears to be one of those unfortunate professions in which when one is not paid for doing it one often does it better. Our aspirations remain undiminished, however, and in time our fantasies become ecstatic: Putting unemployed theologians back to work! What a grand vision and humane service. It might even contribute to the general social welfare, perhaps increase the gross national product! Or at least the dignity of labor. And the challenge is all the greater when one considers that it is not only the unemployed but the employed theologians as well that can be put back to work again on theology. For even the employed theologians have by and large forgotten the baroque crafts and skills of theological artistry in which theologians once used to take such pride. Ending unemployment! What a worthy social vision—considered, of course, purely from a humanitarian point of view.

How might these vital, unemployed energies be put to work? What useful jobs are left to theologians, now that traditional (sacramentally attentive, ecclesiastically responsive, tradition-maintaining) theological tasks appear, from a certain point of view, so *passé?* What can theologians do with themselves as they drink the heady wines of modern freedom? In our reverie, we wonder: Might they actually have some definite calling, some urgent challenge yet to meet, or at least some little errand to run, before their final retirement from active service?

What Else Is New?

What follows is for some readers best to be viewed under the genre of entertainment. It should be tasted, not masticated, more like wine than beef, and if anyone should decide to proceed further it is best to do so in the spirit of penultimate, not ultimate seriousness. For the last thing we need is another serious new *program* of theology. Theological programs (or "programmes") have come and gone at an embarrassing rate in the last two decades, and I would prefer to disclaim any expectations that such might be my purpose. The only program that conceivably might serve some useful function, I suspect, would be a *counterprogrammatic* theology, if that could be imagined, namely, a program whose sole purpose is to end theology programs.

So, if it looks as if I am proposing a reform of theology, that is only half right. Theology does need to be reformed, but not in a new way, only in an old and familiar way. The reform-minded are not likely to gain much comfort from the inverted notions that Christian teaching needs to be reformed in the direction of antiquity, or that modernity is already way out of date, or that the cheap promise of radical newness is the most boring and repetitious of all modern ideas.

I once had a curious dream that rekindled my deepest theological hopes. The only scene I can remember was in the New Haven cemetery, where I accidentally stumbled over my own tombstone only to be confronted by this astonishing epitaph: "He made no new contribution to theology." I was marvelously pleased by the idea and deeply reassured. Why? Because I have of late been trying in my own way to follow the mandate of Irenaeus "not to invent new doctrine." No concept was more deplored by the early ecumenical councils than the notion that theology's task was to "innovate" *(neōterizein),* which to them implied some imagined creative addition to the apostolic teaching, and thus something "other than" *(heteros)* the received doctrine *(doxa),* "the baptism into which we have been baptized." What the church fathers least wished for in a theology was that it would be "fresh," "self-expressive," or an embellishment of purely private inspirations, as if these might stand as some "decisive improvement" on the apostolic teaching. Yet from the first day I ever thought of becoming a theologian I have been earnestly taught that my most urgent task was to "think creatively" and to make "some new contribution" to theology eventually. So you can imagine that it took no small effort to resist the repeated reinforcements of my best education in order to overcome the constant temptation to novelty. And you can understand how relieved I was to see such a lovely epitaph prefigured in a dream.

The present mood of academic theology is boredom. One cannot help wonder, purely out of humane interest, whether there might be some therapy for this boredom. There seems to be no lack of a certain kind of brilliance among some who view themselves as theologians, and plodding persistence among others, but the mind often seems to have lost heart and the body to have lost its soul. Admittedly, theology has managed to gain a modest status in the world, a chair here or there in an enormous tax-supported university, the sporadic attention of the media (focused selectively on radical politics, homosexuality, and death). For half a century, theology has been earnestly longing and wishing and even praying (well, that might be an exaggeration) for a little more respectability in the eyes of modernity. It has not asked for the moon—even one tiny step up the academic pecking order would be savored immensely. It has developed professional societies that are neat carbon copies of other professional societies. It has even undergone a dramatic name change, from theology to religious studies. It has seemed "a decisive step ahead" to say that its subject matter is no longer strictly speaking God or revelation but the phenomena of religious experience. Even though religion departments remain almost pariahs in some universities, it can be fairly reported that the field of religious studies now holds a slender beachhead in the modern secular university.

This is no small achievement, but has it lead to a sense of fulfillment, integrity, or satisfaction? Apparently not, judged by the depression-proneness and vocational egress rate in this professional sphere. Even amid its apparent secular successes, the question lingers: How is theology to find true happiness in the modern world? Such a theme might even be worthy of an afternoon soap opera. What is theology now to do with its new-found freedom?

Theology today stands in a comic relation to its subject matter. It is the most humorous of all disciplines because it has worked so hard to disavow its distinctive task. Yet despite its hard-working earnestness, contemporary theology has never received the subtle comic treatment it so richly deserves.

Some interpret the dilemma of theology essentially as a grave scarcity of decent causes to advocate. In such a situation, expansive idealism must search ever more desperately to find even a modestly decent cause. Eventually, with gestures of importance, it must resort to the protection of terrorist rights, the graffiti movement, the right to shout profanities in one's grandmother's ear, the natural rights of sharks, and so on. These causes offer challenges only for a short time, but then the excitement seems to wane; and, besides, they so often tend unfortunately to nauseate the very religious constituencies that the exponents would wish to attract, guide, guru, and represent. All this adds up to a "cause gap," which the ensuing discussion does its best to overcome.

Theology and ministry are inevitably concerned with good causes and with the human cause. But the problem is that we have developed some compulsive needs for ever-new causes to fuel our infinitely expansive idealisms. As in the fuel shortage, we burn up causes so fast that they are in very short supply, but we remain hooked on being habitually heavy fuel users.

The Reluctant Advocate

I do not mean to depreciate the importance of advocacy in ministry or to neglect its intricate psychological dynamics. In fact, in moments of deadliest theological boredom, we may even wonder if advocacy of a very different sort might be our emerging task—but advocacy of what? All the best candidates for advocacy seem already to be taken up. Keep in mind that an authentic event of advocacy requires a collusion between two parties, one with a strong protective motive and another with high vulnerability and weakness. So the thought presses on us and furrows our brows: What available victim is most truly weak and vulnerable, most kicked around and despised in the modern world of religious ideas? That may finally be on the track of a solution. Aha! When we put the question in that way, the answer seems surprisingly evident: the cause most despised, ignored, and least well defended in modern times, particularly among intellectuals, is religious orthodoxy. It is most passé, most disinteresting. In fact, it is at the very bottom of the heap of lost causes. So, one might reason, that is where our energies as advocates might really count.

What is an attorney for? To present the client's case and protect her or his rights in the courts regardless of how he or she may feel personally toward the client. Whether the attorney is attracted to the client's smile or repulsed by the client's limp or surliness is irrelevant to the case. The best advocacy ignores personal feelings and states clearly the merits of the case.

Suppose we in ministry were attorneys for ancient ecumenical Christianity in the courts of modernity. Even if there were things about these rascals, the apostles and martyrs, that we personally disliked, language they used that seemed crude to us, habits that revolted us,—still if we were conscientious attorneys solemnly charged with their defense, these personal aversions would be completely set aside, and all our attention would focus on how best to present the merits of their case. Now let us suppose that, in the process of preparing their almost hopeless case for trial, we as attorneys became increasingly convinced against our earlier predispositions that they were not only innocent, but that the proper advocacy of their case was of utmost importance to society and even to the human future. Would not we study diligently and prepare ourselves in detail for every possible contingency in argument and be able to answer all the spurious invectives that would understandably be hurled at our clients? And suppose we had discovered that both judge and jury were already predisposed to view them with suspicion and discount their testimony. Would not we be compelled to work all the harder to obtain the best evidence on behalf of our clients, even though the evidence against them at times seemed overwhelming? For let us suppose that we as attorneys have become all the more firmly persuaded of their innocence and rightness the more deeply we delve into the case, even though at first we could hardly stand the odor of their breath or the strangeness of their language. Step by step, we must establish the credibility of our witnesses, answer charges against our clients, prove that they could not have done all the damage they are accused of, and vindicate them.

and vigorous, if it is to obtain a fair trial.

The operating assumption of this analogy is that persons in ministry have already made a prior decision to uphold authentic Christian teaching. We are duty bound to give this advocacy a good try. But we continue to put ourselves in the role of the bad lawyer—demanding credentials and advanced payments from our clients, rather than placing on ourselves the requirement of discovering the actual merits of their case. It is apparent that on some occasions a good lawyer may defend a disreputable client—but presumably we in ministry have already made a fundamental decision about the good character of our client. What else could our ordination imply? Yet we are still saying to our clients that they must pay us first, and then we will see later if they happen to be of sufficient character that they deserve our defense.

Theology as Fashion

Try another fantasy. Suppose Christian teaching were considered essentially under the category of fashion. That in fact seems to be the way much "media theology" has functioned in the last quarter century, searching breathlessly for the next new mushroom in the meadow. And we in ministry have colluded with it. Much of the energy of Christian teaching recently has gone into the effort, first, to achieve a kind of predictive sociological expertise about what is the "next new cultural wave" coming (politically, psychologically, artistically, philosophically, whatever), and then, having spotted an "emergent movement" cresting in the distance, to see if we might get some small foothold for Christianity on that rolling bandwagon so we can enjoy at least a brief ride as long as it lasts.

Does this describe recent theology fairly? Again and again when I have asked audiences of pastors that question, I have been reassured that the description is not at all unfair. It seems accurate to me, since I have experienced myself fairly often as working unconsciously just in this way. Process theology and existential theology are prototype examples, where vast theological programs emerge to try to bend the tradition to accommodate to a Whitehead or Heidegger, and at those points where the tradition does not easily accommodate it is pronounced (note the absolute self-assurance of this act of condemnation) "irrelevant to the modern mind," lost from the "intellectual momentum of our times."

Returning to the fantasy, suppose theology were fashion and we were fashion designers. Let us go all the way and imagine that we are in the company of Yves Saint Laurent, Pierre Cardin, Givenchy, and Dior, assembled in Paris to discuss possibilities for next year's theological market. Suppose we, sensing a crisis of boredom, had set our heads on inventing some astonishing novelty in theology. What would be the most novel, unheard-of, and outrageous new possibility for modern theology? It is quite evident: orthodoxy. We would say: Is it not about time for a reappearance of orthodoxy? Why? Well, because the excesses of rapid change in our industry almost require it, because people are becoming tired of everything that has paraded itself before them for decades as ever more frenetically modern and even more up to date than the last up-to-date thing. It is clear, since all that has become tiresome, that the least modern option is now our best bet, and that, by definition, is orthodoxy. In fact, one might say, with a wink, if theological fashion is to recover, it *must* turn to orthodoxy.

The point of our analogy is not to show that Christian theology is like fashion or that it should begin with market research, but rather that even if it is conceived only on this lowest level of critical sensitivity, at some point the designers would have to come full circle back to the classical models. But Christian teaching, of course, is least understood when it is conceived as fashion. Fashion appeals to the spirit of novelty; Christianity transmutes the very idea of novelty.

I have been confidentially taken aside and gently warned by worried friends that my recent fixation on ancient ecumenical orthodoxy is really . . . well, let's face it, intolerable. Orthodoxy by *any* other name would smell much sweeter. They have cautioned me that the whole idea is unmarketable, will have no effect, and will be wasted effort. They have anxiously pleaded with me to say whatever curious or crazy thing I have to say but, please, in some language less embarrassing to the modern consensus than that of orthodoxy.

All this is amusing. Whether orthodoxy is high or low on a Nielsen chart strikes me as a subject for an vaudeville act or an extended situation comedy. Classical Christianity has always been far less concerned with high acceptance ratings among its human audiences (even with esteemed academic audiences) than with its single divine auditor. This does not imply that Christianity should masochistically wish for low ratings or hope desperately to be ignored, as it has on some occasions, but neither can it congratulate itself on the fleeting applause of the majority if that should imply a backdoor sellout of its historical memory.

Rather than prudishly stomping away from this vaudeville show or abruptly switching off this situation comedy, (the popularity rating of orthodoxy), I would prefer to watch it play for a while and see whether it might be unexpectedly entertaining. Suppose we imagine a theologian, fresh out of graduate school, who has determined to begin the construction of a massive new doctrinal system solely on the basis of extensive market research into the needs and hungers of the current cultural audience. (Don't laugh; it could be done.) The samples are meticulously gathered and calculated, fed into the computer, and the results eagerly awaited. (Yes, I admit the premise is ridiculous, because it turns theology into something that it decidedly is not—namely, public opinion analysis and salesmanship—but bear with me and see if we can learn something even from a disreputable premise.) Now our focus will be an assessment of the current cultural momentum as the sole basis of doctrinal definition. Our young genius double-checks his figures to see if they are correct. A surprising readout is beginning to burp out of the computer. It indicates that there apparently exists a deep itch in our society to settle things down, ask how things got this way, recover our identities, and see if we might be able to conserve and renew our more stable moral, political, and religious traditions. Further examination of these data reveals something more than a minor trend to nostalgia or sentimentality, the subtle influence of some incipient fascist trend in politics, or the validation of some backlash theory. They appear to reveal an immense appetite for historical identity and roots in a compulsively mobile society whose magic words are *change, new, now,* and *breakthrough.*

He runs the punch cards back through the computer thinking that it might have made a mistake, perhaps a reversal of key components of the equation. But no, on second run again it is confirmed: The actual audience for our new theological construct is amazingly different from the one we thought was there on the basis of our listening to Bultmann's description of "modern man," Tillich's concept of "correlation" with the "kairos" of our times, or the process theologians' estimates of the *Zeitgeist.* All these standard portrayals render a profile of an audience that is extremely dissatisfied with the encumbrances of tradition, insatiably thirsting for "fundamental change" based on a wholly this-worldly rejection of all supernaturalisms and so on. Our clever young theologian then discovers to his astonishment that other eminent public opinion analysts—Gallup, Harris, Yankelovich—are all coming up with similar conclusions. The actual audience being discovered out there is one that is preeminently characterized by the hunger for continuity, stability, the freedom to sustain and enhance traditional values, historical identifications, and old-fashioned ways. This comes as quite a shock, because we were prepared to construct a quite different theological system based on a different expected audience profile, so it seems that a great deal of our preliminary work must now be thrown out and redone.

The "Movement" Theologian

In order to sharpen our portrayal of theology's amiable accommodation to modernity, I will describe a particular individual, an ordained theologian whom I have known for a long time, whose career in some sense can only be described as that of a "movement person." If I appear to go into needless detail about this person, it is nonetheless useful to get some sense of the specifics of what we mean by an *addictive accommodationism.* In all his pursuit of movements, his overall pattern was diligently to learn from them, to throw himself into them, and then eventually to baptize them as if they were identical with the Christian center.

Now in his mid-forties, our subject took his first plunge into "movement identity" almost thirty years ago when, at sixteen, he joined the United World Federalists to promote world government through various educational and church groups. From 1953 (when he attended the Evanston Assembly) to 1966 (at the Geneva consultation on Christianity and the Social Order), he was involved in ecumenical debate, promotion, and organization. His deepening involvement in the civil rights movement began at about seventeen, later intensified by his attendance of the national NAACP convention in 1953 and by subsequent participation in marches, demonstrations, pray-ins, sit-ins, letter campaigns, and other forms of political activism.

More than a decade before the Vietnam War, our "movement theologian" was an active pacifist, struggling to motivate the antiwar movement during the difficult McCarthy days. The fact that he understood himself as a democratic socialist and theoretical Marxist during the McCarthy period did not make his task any easier. He spearheaded the first Students for Democratic Action group to be organized in his conservative home state in the early 1950s. By the mid-1950s, he was active in the American Civil Liberties Union; in the pre-1960s women's rights movement, as an advocate of liberalized abortions; and as an opponent of state's rights, military spending, and bourgeois morality. His movement identity took a new turn in the late 1950s, when he became enamored with the existentialist movement, immersing himself particularly in the demythologization movement, writing his doctoral disseration on its chief theorist.

The early 1960s found him intimately engaged in the client-centered therapy movement. Later he became engrossed in Transactional Analysis and soon was actively participating in the Gestalt therapy movement, especially through Esalen connections. His involvement deepened in the "third force" movement in humanistic psychology, struggling to move beyond psychoanalysis and behaviorism, as he contributed to its journals, and experimented with its therapeutic strategies in his theological school classrooms. This was supplemented by a several years involvement in the T-Group movement associated with the National Training Laboratories, which he tried to integrate into his religious views. In the early 1970s, he joined a society for the study of paranormal phenomena, taught a class in parapsychology, and directed controlled research experiments with mung beans, Kirlian photography, biorhythm charts, pyramids, tarot cards, and the correlation of astrological predictions with the daily ups and downs of behavior.

My purpose in reciting this long litany is not to boast, for indeed I am that wandering theologian, less proud than amused by the territory I have covered. Rather, the purpose is to recite a straightforward description of what at least one theologian conceived to be his task in successive phases of the last three decades. So when I am speaking of a diarrhea of religious accommodation, I am not thinking of "the other guys" or speaking in the abstract, but out of my own personal history. I do not wish contritely to apologize for my thirty years as a movement person, because I learned so much and encountered so many bright and beautiful persons. But I now experience the afterburn of "movement" existence, of messianic pretensions, of self-congratulatory idealism. It is understandable after this roller-coaster ride, that I would be drawn to a "postmovement" sociology of continuity, maintenance, and legitimation, hoping to ameliorate the "movement psychology" of immediate change. The very thinkers I once excoriated as "conservative" (the Burkes, the Newmans, the

Neo-Thomists) I now find annually increasing in plausibility, depth, and wisdom.

The shocker is not merely that I rode every bandwagon in sight, but that I thought I was doing Christian teaching a marvelous favor by it, and at times considered it the very substance of the Christian teaching office. While Christian teaching must not rule out any investigations of truth or active involvement to embody it, we should be wary lest we reduce Christian doctrine to these movements and should be better prepared to discern which movements are more or less an expression of Christ's ministry to the world.

It was the abortion movement, more than anything else, that brought me to movement revulsiveness. The climbing abortion statistics made me movement weary, movement demoralized. I now suspect that a fair amount of my own idealistic history of political action was ill conceived by self-deceptive romanticisms, in search of power in the form of prestige, that were from the beginning willing to destroy human traditions in the name of humanity, and at the end willing to extinguish the futures of countless unborn children in the name of individual autonomy. So, reflected in the mirror of my own history, I see my own generation and my children's generation of movement idealisms as naively proud and sadly misdirected, despite good intentions. If I have grown wary about movement people, it is because I am wary of the consequences of my own good intentions.

Meanwhile, my intellectual dialogue has been embarrassingly constricted to university colleagues and liberal churchmen. When I discover among brilliant Roman Catholic, neo-evangelical, and Jewish brothers and sisters a marvelous depth of historical and moral awareness, I wonder why it has taken me so long to discover them, what was it about my liberal

Christian tradition that systematically cut me off from dialogue with them, and why my tradition has been so defensive toward them. All these questions are subjects for further historical and sociological investigation, but they arise out of a vague sense of grief over lost possibilities and out of confusion that a tradition that spoke so often about tolerance and universality could be so intolerant and parochial.

2

Full Circle

I USE the term *modernity* in the same sense that many Frenchmen speak of *modernité* with a wave of the hand and upturned eyes, as something between "gauche" and "compulsive up-to-dateness." The Germans use the term *Modernität* in a similarly pejorative way. I do not mean to ignore all the scientific and political achievements of the modern period but rather to point to one of our consistently worst habits as modern persons, the exaltation of the *modo,* the "just now," the most recent thing, as an unparalleled virtue. This linguistic tendency is found even in the eighteenth-century definition of the modernist as a maintainer of the superiority of modern over ancient literature (and long before anticipated by the fourteenth-century debates about *via moderna,* the "modern way" of the nominalists who denied reality to universal concepts and paved the way for the disintegration of medieval scholasticism.)

Modernity: How Long Will We Tolerate Its Illusions?

The faddism of theology in the past two decades was not accidental—it was necessary *if* you understand theology to be a constant catch-up process, trying to keep pace with each new ripple of the river. What else could theology become but faddist, under such a definition?

The same addiction that has degenerated modern art has also infected theology. The marvelous tradition of Cézanne, Braque, Picasso, and Chagall has of late withered into a speedway race of faddists who have placed such a high value on "doing something different" (no matter what) that creativity has been lost in the frantic search for novelty. An inversion of value has occurred in which the highest value is placed not on artistic imagination, craft, meaning, excellence, or beauty, but on simple novelty, sheer uniqueness. The more outrageous it becomes, the more "creative" it is viewed by some connoisseurs, and the more boring it is to most of us. When novelty becomes the chief criterion of artistic achievement, we can only chuckle at the expensive wool that is being pulled over someone's eyes.

Exactly the same has happened in theology, with its "new theologies" every spring book season, a wide assortment of "new moralities," "new hermeneutics," and (note how the adjectives suddenly have to be pumped up) "revolutionary breakthroughs in political theology." On closer inspection, however, we find that all these views may be found in the books of fifty and a hundred years ago, (except then with mercifully fewer pretensions and less hysteria).

We have blithely proceeded on the skewed assumption that in theology—just as in corn poppers, electric toothbrushes, and automobile exhaust systems—new is good, newer is better, and newest is best. The correction of this skewed analogy will have a shocking effect on seminaries now long habituated to instant theology. The comic–tragic irony is that these "most innovative" seminaries are regarded in certain circles as better just to that degree that they follow this debilitating assumption. So the "best" ones have by this logic cut themselves systematically off from any sustained discourse with classical Christianity, or have at least tended to do so. But if we in liberal Protestantism should learn again to work at the distinction between heterodoxy and orthodoxy, what effect would it have on pastoral care, Christian education, preaching, biblical studies, administrative oversight, social ethics, and so on? The possibilities are staggering.

The central theme of contemporary theology is accommodation to modernity. It is the underlying motif that unites the seemingly vast differences between existential theology, process theology, liberation theology, demythologization, and many varieties of liberal theology—all are searching for some more compatible adjustment to modernity.

The spirit of accommodation has not prevailed without occasional minority voices and skirmishes, but the resistance to it has been sporadic, divided, and defensive: Some pre-Vatican II Roman Catholic holdouts and a few lonely Anglo-Catholics have given some token resistance to the wholesale accommodation of Christianity to modernity, but they often send signals that reveal their self-understanding as living anachronisms. Political and philosophical conservatism has offered some resistance, but it has been unfortunately coupled with political programs that seem to deny much of classical Christianity's concern for the poor. The brief flurry of Barthian–Niebuhrian "neo-orthodoxy" never gained much grass-roots ecclesial strength, and had its influence mainly in a few key seminaries. Advocates of verbal inerrancy of scripture have been more effective in nurturing intergenerational communities of faith, but their influence has been local and regional, and they have hardly affected the vast cities of modernity.

Pacifist sects such as the Amish have literally withdrawn from modernity and will have nothing to do with it. No cars, no condoms, no buttons, no mass media, and so on. Even if we should admire their spirit and tenacity, we are far too habituated to the technologies and assumptions of modernity to join them on their rigorous path.

A more influential model for postmodern orthodox Christians are postmodern orthodox Jews. Often the sons and daughters of immigrants who gave enormous energies to finding their way into American upward mobility, the present generation has tripped radically into the far edges of modern experimental consciousness, only eventually to find their way back into the marvelous Jewish heritage that their grandfathers had to suppress temporarily and at times disavow.

Like young Jews, young Christians are trying to become astute gardeners of their tradition, learning to transplant the ancient faith in the fresh soil of modernity. They have learned, however, that some of the seeds spuriously marketed as "Christian" in the modern ideological supermarket produce a quite different fruit from the seeds they are now trying to nurture from a few remaining plants that have endured through the ravages of modernity. They are carefully tending, cultivating, and learning how to protect the rare plants that come from these genuine seeds that differ so completely from the tasteless, fabricated modern claimants.

The agenda for theology in the last quarter of the twentieth century, following the steady deterioration of a hundred years and the disaster of the last two decades, is to begin to prepare the postmodern Christian community for its third millennium by returning again to the careful study and respectful following of the central tradition of classical Christianity. It will require energetic historical inquiry into the internal reasonings of classical Christian orthodoxy, a new gift of empathy for alternative forms of historical consciousness, an ability to discern what is and what is not within the core. Ministry will have to learn anew a skill that once was taken for granted but now has become long forgotten, the ability to distinguish between doctrinal authenticity and phoniness. It is a question we have too long pretended did not exist, and if we do not take it up soon our grandchildren will find it ever more difficult.

The Approach of the Third Millennium

Instead of modernity discrediting Christian faith as advertised, modernity itself is unexpectedly in the process of being discredited. The shallows of modernity only make it more urgent to explore the depths of Christian hope and love. We have overassessed modernity's power to deliver and underassessed its inner contradictions and limits. Out of that vast miscalculation, the advocates of modernity in every generation since Voltaire have repeatedly announced the imminent demise of religion. One would think that this tiresome prognostication would at some time finally be ignored. It was not until the last quarter century that professors and ministers of religion in fairly large numbers began to cast their lot with the prognosis of Voltaire. Yet, far from disposing of Christian orthodoxy, modernity has now come full circle. Against all its self-expectations it is now having to face up to its own interpersonal bankruptcy, social neuroses, and moral vacuity.

The religious challenge to young people today as we approach Christianity's third millennium is to end the defensive mentality of retreat and failure of nerve in the presence of a rapidly deteriorating modern ethos that has lost its moral power. Increasing numbers of them are no longer willing to buy into the assumption that modernity holds a legitimate moral authority over Christian conscience.

If classical Christian consciousness should become temporarily lost and obliterated, it would be modernity's loss as well as Christianity's. For even the secularization process has tended to receive its moral vitality from its constant companion, Christianity. If we should ever imagine that modernity's suffering might be lessened by the retreat of Christianity from its central convictions, we would have misunderstood modernity as badly as we have Christianity. If we should ever in moments of demoralization fantasize that the finest contribution Christianity could make to modernity would be to abandon its oldest traditions (against which a frustrated modernity has always had to struggle), then we should fear most not for the fate of Christianity (the continuity of whose Word God himself has promised to assure) but of modernity without Christianity's compassionate realism.

An awareness is dawning : It is time to quit our sniveling apologies for the distortions of traditional Christianity and go right back to the scriptural and patristic texts to ask how classical Christianity itself might teach us to understand the providence of God in the midst of our modern situation. This is why our students are reading classical Christian interpretations of history (from Augustine's *City of God* through Calvin and Milton to Kierkegaard's *The Present Age)* with far greater urgency today than they were reading pop modern chauvinist interpreters of history such as Alvin Toffler, Harvey Cox, or Malcolm Boyd a few years ago. By "modern chauvinist" I mean those whose historical perspective, loyalties, and attachments are so strictly limited to modern values that they impulsively denigrate all premodern wisdoms.

Christianity does not rejoice in the failure of modernity. But neither does Christianity need to assume that its destiny is ultimately bound up with the failure or success of modernity. It is just because we have tried to become successful on modernity's terms that we have contracted theological vertigo. It is not surprising that we should now be quietly mourning the loss of our own surest form of accountability to modernity, which is faithfulness to the scriptural tradition that from the beginning has provided the deepest spiritual wellsprings of modern consciousness.

Classical Christianity has never said that the believer cannot inquire into the scientific understanding of reality or probe the edges of undiscovered truth or refine the methods of research to the tiniest caliber; rather, it has celebrated the hope that all the new dimensions of truth awaiting our discovery are more profoundly understandable and make wiser sense within the frame of reference of the meaning of universal history. This meaning Christians believe to be revealed in Jesus. There is nothing in the orthodox Jewish or Christian tradition that prohibits the modern mind from feeding its computers with the most complex data, sorting out the conflicted energies of the human psyche, refining the methods of historical investigation, or experimenting with the expansion of consciousness through meditation. These are rather to be viewed with great joy, especially when seen in relation to the end of history, which for Christians and Jews is ultimately expected as an event of resurrection beyond all human alienations.

By "classical Christianity (or ancient ecumenical orthodoxy)," I mean the Christian consensus of the first millennium. A fuller statement of that consensus awaits Chapter 5, but we must ask, in a preliminary way, What is orthodoxy? In brief, is that to which Vincent of Lerins pointed in the phrase *quod ubique, quod semper, quod ab omnibus creditum est* ("that which has been everywhere and always and by everyone believed") the faith generally shared by all Christians, especially as defined in the crucial early period of Christian doctrinal definition. These definitions were not written by individuals but were hammered out by synods, councils, and consensual bodies. On at least seven notable occasions, they met on a worldwide basis to express the universal consent of Christianity to the apostolic teaching as defined—the seven ecumenical councils that have been accepted by the church in all its branches as normative for at least its first one and a half millennia.

The seven councils commonly held both in East and West as binding on all Christians, both having and deserving universal Christian consent, are (with dates and chief subjects): (1) Nicaea (325, Arianism); (2) Constantinople I (381, Apollinariansim); (3) Ephesus (431, Nestorianism); (4) Chalcedon (451, Eutychianism); (5) Constantinople II (553, Three Chapters Controversy); (6) Constantinople III (680–681, Monothelitism); and (7) Nicaea II (787, Iconoclasm). We might be led to assume that every ordained minister would be thoroughly schooled in the canons and decrees of these universally accepted councils (to be presupposed as one assumes that the multiplication tables are known by every mathematician), but that would be a rash assumption. A thorough reappraisal of the theological method implicit in these early doctrinal formulations is crucially a part of the awaiting agenda of contemporary theology.

The Fragile Assumptions of Modernity

The most basic theological decisions the pastor makes are often unnoticed, under the surface, even unconscious. One only notices much later how crucial they are. Our relation to modernity is just such a fate-laden precognitive decision. Consciously or not, every Christian teacher must decide how much legitimacy he is willing to grant the assumptions of modernity, how deeply he will or will not allow himself to be intimidated by them, and how powerfully they will shape his perception of the Christian faith.

Keep in mind that many Christians have existed prior to modernity, so surely it cannot be concluded that the assumptions of modernity are essential to or definitive for Christian faith. The question is to what extent the assumptions of modernity are even compatible with Christian faith.

Modernity is less a time than an ideological place. It is less a period than an attitude. Although it has had many premodern manifestations, it was not until the nineteenth century that it began to expand from the pockets of the intelligentsia into general circulation in Western society. By the twentieth century, attitudes that had been considered odd and disreputable in previous periods had become the *Zeitgeist* of which the secular university now considers itself the conscience and guide. By the last quarter of this century, the modern university has become less and less an *universitas* in the classical sense and more and more an exponent and apologist for the mentality of modernity.

If we insist on bandying about the term *modernity,* the reader has a right to ask for a clearer definition of the particular way we are using it, even if it may be a definition that not everyone would agree on. The term *modernity* has several strata of meanings in this book that might be compared to a target of three concentric circles with a bullseye. The outer, more general circle refers to modernity in the wider sense of the overarching intellectual ideology of a historical period lasting from the French Revolution to the present. It is a period whose general features (optimism, scientific humanism, narcissistic hedonism, naturalistic reductionism, and individualism) have been well described by modern intellectual historians such as Peter Gay, Basil Willey, Crane Brinton, Herbert Randall, and Paul Tillich, and whose sociological features have been accurately delineated by writers such as Robert Lifton, David Riesman, Kenneth Boulding, Philip Slater, and Peter Berger. These are descriptions of modernity that our discussion need not recount but (importantly) presupposes.

The second, intermediate circle of our target defines modernity more tightly as a mentality, found especially among certain intellectual elites, which assumes that chronologically recent ways of knowing the truth are self-evidently superior to all premodern alternatives. Religious thought of the last two decades has been particularly susceptible to taking their opinion with engrossed seriousness, as if their fantasies were important to the future of Christianity and of all humankind.

The inner circle or bullseye of our target, however, is modernity in the sense of a later-stage deterioration of both of the preceding viewpoints. It is a more recent intensification of the dilemmas of modern consciousness that have accelerated generally over the last half century, but that in the last two decades have reached a dramatic moment of precipitous moral decline. It is only in the 1960s and 1970s that the bitter fruits of modernity, which have been two centuries in the making, have been widely grasped, eaten, gorged, disgorged, and found socially undigestible. This, on a fairly large social scale, is an event of the last two decades.

No simple table can do justice to the rich complexities of historical development, yet the function of a table is to capture the most simple and evident categories of a problem for introductory clarification. It is with this hope that I attempt, in the schema on page 38, to sort out the major differences between premodern, modern, and postmodern consciousness.

The rhetoric of unrestrained individual freedom is a prominent earmark of the spirit of modernity. The goal of modern life is to be liberated from restrictions, constraints, traditions, and all social parenting—all of which is self-evidently presumed to be dehumanizing. "If we were only free from *x* or *y*," modernity fantasizes, "then we could truly be ourselves." So the social, psychological, and political strategies and rhetoric of modernity all focus on a highly abstract notion of individual freedom, abstract because it is taken away from *(abs- + trahere)* its matrix of social accountability. The hunger of freedom to actualize itself quite individually is the despair of modernity, for authentic freedom exists only amid covenant responsibility. So the freedom of which modernity speaks is seldom authentic freedom, but a yearning, self-negating "fallen" freedom that can only despairingly imagine itself to be free.

Sustained covenant accountability is forgotten in the interest of subjective self-expression. The social result is precisely the inordinate, hedonic self-assertiveness that Jewish and Christian ethics have always eschewed as the center of the human predicament, the *yetzer ha-ra* (evil inclination). Its horrifying consequences are often not recognized until we have on our hands a world at war, unchecked compulsivity, a polluted atmosphere, or an impending genocide. Then we get worried

	PREMODERN ERAS *(Prior to Eighteenth century)*	MODERNITY *(Eighteenth, Nineteenth, and Twentieth centuries)*	LATER-STAGE MODERNITY *(Third quarter of Twentieth century)*	POSTMODERNITY *(Embryonic, awakening, preparing to enter the third millennium)*
WESTERN HISTORICAL EXPERIENCE:	The Western intellectual and cultural traditions from Judeo-Christian and Greco-Roman antiquity to the Enlightenment	Rise of autonomous individualism, demystification, secularization, naturalistic reductionism, scientific empiricism, historical criticism	Precipitous deterioration of social processes under tutelage of radical autonomous individualism, narcissistic hedonism, naturalistic reductionism	Hunger for means of social maintenance, continuity, parenting, intergenerational traditioning, historical awareness, freedom from the repressions of modernity
CHRISTIAN THEOLOGICAL TRADITION:	Patristic, medieval, and reformation theologies, all of which adhered to the doctrines of the seven ecumenical councils, the orthodox consensus of the first Christian millennium; = classical Christianity	Rise of pietism, religious individualism, liberalism, theologies of religious experience, scientific study of religion, social gospel, neo-orthodoxy, fundamentalism, modern ecumenism, existentialism, and process theology; = classical Christian symbols modernized, reinterpreted, demythologized, psychologized	Accelerating hunger for acceptance by modernity; centerless accommodation to assumptions of modernity in rapidly deteriorating phase; = classical Christian language debased yet without awareness of debasement	The possibility of postmodern orthodoxy, having been immersed in the deteriorations of later stage modernity, now reawakened to the power and beauty of classical Christianity, seeking to incorporate the achievements of modernity into an ethos and intellectus that transcends modernity under the guidance of ancient ecumenical Christianity

and wonder what could possibly have gone wrong.

Modernity is chiefly distinguished by a predisposed contempt for premodern ideas, a vague boredom in the face of the heroic struggles of primitive and historical human communities, a diffuse disrespect for the intellectual, social, and moral achievements of all previous periods. Some might object that it is only to be expected of any society, and not modernity only, that its egocentricity would tend toward disrespect of all other social norms and intellectual ideas. This is disproved by the awesome respect that some societies have shown for their ancestor's traditions and for social structures and ideas prior to them.

A related distinction between late modern and postmodern consciousness hinges on attitudes toward *parenting.* Late modern consciousness sees most social parenting as alienating by definition. Institutional structures are viewed as inimical to individuated human freedom. No responsibility is felt for the nurture of social continuities or multigenerational moral tradition. The struggle is for individual autonomy *against* social repressions. Overweening hope is pinned on the personal moral competence of the individual who is expected single-handedly to reconstruct the human situation better than any social tradition ever could have. This is why the modern period generally expresses the psychological quality of the *adolescent's* struggle against oppressive parenting and against historical wisdom of all sorts. Surely every adolescent needs at times to struggle for his or her own individual autonomy against parental dependencies, but when this mentality becomes a total world view, political ethic, psychological strategy, and interpersonal posture, it fails to understand the legitimate functions of tradition maintenance and historical reasoning. Nothing is more characteristic of post modern consciousness than the willingness to be parented by historical reason and by the wisdom of social experience.

These are the axial assumptions of later-stage modernity: contempt for premodern wisdoms, the absolutizing of the values of autonomous individualism, awed deference to reductionistic naturalism and scientific empiricism as the final court of appeal in truth questions, the adolescent refusal of parenting, an optimistic evolutionary historical progessivism linked uncomfortably with the most unabashed forms of narcissistic hedonism. This is a sketchy profile of the ideology of modernity (as we are using the term) which could easily be amplified by listening to the underlying assumptions of the usual conversations of the "happy hours" of modernity.

Unfolding modern history is embarrassing precisely these axioms. Not some theory, but actual modern *history.* We need only mention Auschwitz, My-Lai, Solzhenitsyn's *Gulag Archipelago, Screw* magazine, the assault statistics in public schools, the juvenile suicide rate, or the heroin epidemic to point to the depth of the failure of modern consciousness. While modernity continues blandly to teach us that we are moving ever upward and onward, the actual history of late modernity is increasingly brutal, barbarian, and malignant.

The Sellout

Why then do religious types still persist in thinking that they have a winner in modernity? Because we have been so deeply ensconced in the progressivist illusion that modernity *by definition* inevitably must be a winner. So it is impossible for us even to hear the count when we are down. The idealized self-image of modernity compulsively requires that we put on enormous blinders to prevent serious glimpses into challenging premodern wisdoms. We cannot learn from their failures and achievements because we have already predecided that we in our chronological "superiority" (later = better) have nothing of importance to learn from them. This is reflected in the prevailing assumption that any textbook written more than ten years ago *must* be out of date (an assumption more true for physics than theology). These oppressive tendencies have held mesmerizing power over the intellectual leadership to which religious communities have looked wistfully for guidance in recent years. It is just this progressivist assumption that postmodern consciousness is no longer willing to abide. Yet the courage to resist that assumption cannot easily emerge from within the very sphere in which that assumption exerts absolute control. That sphere is what we are calling *modernity*. Modernity is not just a time, but a set of passions, hopes, and ideas, a mentality that prevails in some circles more than in others.

The philosophical center of modernity is no dark secret. It is an easily recognized, thoroughgoingly narcissistic hedonism that assumes that moral value is reducible to cash value and sensory experience. It views human existence essentially as spiritless body, sex as depersonalized vaginal ingress, psychology as amoral data gathering, and politics as the manipulation of power. It systematically ignores the human capacity for self-transcendence, moral reasoning, covenant commitment, and self-sacrificial agape.

These axiomatic assumptions prevail among the intellectual elite that has of late become the apple of many a parson's eye. While the religious leadership should have been giving them what it distinctively has to give—namely, firm, critical resistance rooted in an historical perspective that modernity could find instructive—instead the religious leadership withheld its gift and whored after each successive stage of modernity's journey. While its lusty affair with modernity has been going on for about two centuries, it has not been until the last quarter century that there has been a wholesale devaluation of the currency of Christian language, symbolism, teaching, and witness.

Young people in ministry are beginning to be vaguely aware of the depth of the sellout, the urgency to redirect the momentum and the fatefulness of their calling to ministry at this nexus of history. The collusions are intricate. A fair amount of courage is required even to face the problem.

The Reversal

Most congregations include worshippers whose basic outlook is conservative and others who are liberal, with varying perspectives in between. It is crucial for us in ministry to understand historically the dynamics that motivate both types. Each has its own psychological hungers, sociological assumptions, and ideological rationales. It is a perennial challenge to pastoral care to learn to participate empathically in the frustrations and anxieties of both. A sensitive pastoral theology will try to resist the tendency to exaggerate either tradition at the expense of renewal or renewal at the expense of tradition. Yet there are moments in the historical process when one needs greater emphasis than the other.

The image of a self-correcting pendulum may help us grasp the way in which the Christian community is constantly seeking an equilibrium of tradition and renewal. The direction of the church's teaching is continuously swinging, as a huge pendulum would swing, between the two extreme apexes of archaism and accommodationism. Since it is swinging through lengthy historical epochs, its motion is often imperceptible to those who have lost historical consciousness. On the right (conservative) side, it tries not to get so fixated archaically on tradition that it cannot behold contemporary challenges, and when it approaches that extreme right apex, the social intuition is to push away from introverted archaism. When, over a period of years, the archaism is temporarily overcome, the pendulum moves ever so slowly (not abruptly as modern change-agent ideologies imagine) toward the left (accommodative) side. Just when one might think that it has moved too far, it touches the apex of extreme cultural accommodation, and then slowly you feel the pull of the community back toward its center of gravity, which is the proclamation of God's steadfast love in Christ addressed to ever-changing human environments.

Where are we today in terms of that analogy? In the last quarter century, we have swung so far to a leftward fixation on change that there is a diffuse, gut-level cultural awareness of the urgent need to find the way back to the center again.

Suppose we existed instead in a different historical period, such as the seventeenth century, in which classical Christianity had been fairly well assimilated and in fact had substantially ossified. Then enlightenment Christianity might have made more historical sense. We would be putting our shoulders to the other side of the pendulum to move it leftward toward relevance and engagement with the world, resisting the rigidities that prevent an engagement with contemporaneity. But we do not live in such a period, and those who think we do are badly mistaken. Christianity does not now need to restate the rhetoric of homeless freedom, which is already overstated in our culture.

We are now struggling on the accommodative apex to understand our particular calling in discrete situations. If at times I may seem to push too hard toward the center, it is because the theological majority still happily proceeds as if their leftward apex were in fact the legitimate center. So in relation to them we may have to resort to rhetoric that itself may be momentarily excessive in order to respond realistically to a prevailing excess.

Although I have used the analogy of a lifeless mechanism, it refers to a history of responsible freedom that moves intermittently between its two apexes in a dynamic rhythm, never coming to a stop. If a pendulum stopped, it would be useless and meaningless. It is only useful when it is in motion, working with tension-filled polarities. And such is theology, existing as it does between tradition and renewal, between apostolicity and contemporaneity, a tension that will never end as long as the church is in history.

We have been so thoroughly habituated by modernity to see the world with historical blinders that we cannot imagine that the hegemony of modernity could ever fizzle. That lack of imagination is the despair of liberalism. Ironically, therefore those *best* trained by modernity are the *least* prepared for the consequences of modernity, and for the hazards of the postmodern future that are already hard upon us.

If we had not already been existing in a situation of excess, the temptations of excessive response would not be so great. But we should not be too surprised if seemingly exaggerated responses seem to be temporarily required in order to effect the directional change that our analogy implies. Some polemical strength and toughness may be needed in order to unveil the moral impotence of the waning modernist momentum.

What we have obviously missed in this pivotal moment of turnaround is the practiced moral judgment of classical Christianity and the theological method of orthodox doctrinal definition, which we might well have been learning from the fourth-century fathers or even from the thirteenth- or seventeenth-century scholastics, had we remembered that they have been here before.

Once having regained this balance, we hope we can then proceed to renew the tradition and attend to its relevant updating. But we cannot renew something we have not yet met. We cannot expand a tradition we have never appropriated. So we must go back to the basics and learn from those most able to teach, namely, the prophets, apostles, saints, and martyrs, in their own language, unhedged by convenient rationalizations.

This continuing tension of pendular movement between polarities is intrinsic to the structure of Jewish and Christian sociology, for the God of Jewish and Christian celebration is involved in history. That necessarily implies a creative tension between the tradition and the changing shapes and sounds of human culture. The development of doctrine does not mean changing the substance of doctrine in each new age but does mean addressing the received tradition to the changing vitalities of each new historical situation. The perennial challenge of ministry is to learn to deal with this tension both imaginatively and faithfully, neglecting neither the authenticity of the tradition or the actual conditions of the emergent world. This is the challenge that Augustine, Maimonides, Nicolas of Cusa, Luther, and Buber all shared in extremely varied historical settings.

But are we describing a momentum that has already turned around or one that will depend on us to turn it around? On the whole, the culture is already in the process of reversal, yet in some locales the reversal is totally unrecognized (this is especially true in the universities), while in other locales it is already beginning to be an accomplished fact.

The reversal of the pendulum's direction today is best understood both as a gift and a task. The reversal is occurring by God's grace, but we at times are also called to help or to let it happen. It is occurring beyond our own specific personal individual spheres, but it sometimes addresses our personal sphere in its particular definiteness. The reversal occurs at the juncture of providence and human freedom, grace and volition, denying neither, affirming both.

The fact that there is sociological, statistical, and public opinion analysis support for the assertion that the direction is in fact reversing brings us a new temptation: to stand on the basis of a new accommodationism based on a revised assessment of popular momentum. I think there is strong evidence that a vast reversal of consciousness is occurring in our culture that at times seems to have an inevitability of its own. But if we rest easily in this frame of mind and if everyone were to do likewise, then the momentum would soon hesitate. So there is an accompanying moral requirement to push and persuade and work in specific contexts to let or help the momentum reverse and to help others to see the reversal of the momentum. There are moments when we may feel that the corrective is already in the air, already occurring, with or without our consent. That is just the context in which we may be called on in the next moment to exert great energies within our own specific sphere of responsibility to alter the momentum, when "I must do it or no one else will." There may be times when the individual will feel in an exaggerated way that he or she is the only one concerned about this reversal, as Elijah felt under the juniper tree on the way to Horeb. There have been times when I have imagined, in demoralized moments, that I am the only theologian who has despaired as deeply as I have despaired over modernity and the only one who has grasped the radical hope of a postmodern Christian classicism—but that, of course, says much more about me than about the actual situation. With closer attentiveness we learn, as Elijah learned, that there still remain "seven thousand in Israel, all who have not bent the knee to Baal" (1 Kings 19:18).

3

Postmodern Orthodoxy

WHEN a theologian forgets the distinction between heterodoxy and orthodoxy, it is roughly equivalent to a physician forgetting the difference between disease and health, axe and scalpel, or a lawyer forgetting the difference between criminality and *corpus juris*. Yet it is just this distinction that theology has over the past two centuries of alleged progress systematically forgotten how to make. A long chain of regrettable results has followed for pastoral care, biblical studies, preaching, Christian ethics, and the mission of the church.

The Tentative Classification of an Evolving Species

It may sound like hair splitting, but I prefer to distinguish *modernity* from that which conservative Protestants used to call "modernism," in the sense of the application of modern critical historical methods to the study of scripture and tradition.

For there is nothing in the ensuing argument that rejects the wise use of historical criticism, even though we resist the fantasy that historical criticism will in itself be a vibrant source of spiritual renewal for Christianity. Nor do I mean by modernity what Pope Pius X called "modernism" in *Pascendi Dominici Gregis* (1907) as "an alliance between faith and false philosophy" arising from curiosity and "pride which rouses the spirit of disobedience and demands a compromise between authority and liberty." For, while Pius X viewed modernism essentially as a theological movement, we are speaking of modernity as a more general attitude of secular culture that prevails particularly among intellectuals and that recent theology has gone out of its way to accommodate and emulate.

Our usage of the term *postmodern* is therefore best understood in the light of the special, although not unique, way we are using the term *late modernity.* The postmodern person has been through the best and the worst that modernity has to offer. The postmodern person is looking for something beyond modernity, some source of meaning and value that transcends the assumptions of modernity. Neck deep in the quicksands of modernity, the postmodern mind is now struggling to set itself free. Some of these postmoderns have happened on classical Christianity and experienced themselves as having been suddenly lifted out of these quicksands onto firmer ground. They have then sought to understand the incredible energy and delivering power of Christianity, and, in the process of returning to the classical texts of ancient Christian tradition and scripture, they have begun to discover that the orthodox core of classical Christianity constitutes a powerful, wide-ranging, viable critique of modern consciousness. Who are the postmodern orthodox? These hardy pilgrims who have set their feet on the path of reappropriating classical Christianity have been through the rigors and hazards of the modern consciousness. Many of my students have set out on this pilgrimage. They are now inviting their theological teachers to join them.

It is useful here to make a basic distinction between two types of orthodoxy: *pre-* and *post*modern. Both are schooled in the same scriptural and patristic texts, and both celebrate and embody the same Christ, but one has journeyed through and dwelled in modernity, while the other has not. Postmodern orthodoxy is distinctive not in its essential doctrine, but in its historical experience. It has been deeply impacted by the modern sociology, physics, psychology, and, more so, by modern history, which premodern orthodoxy has either avoided or by historical accident never had a chance to meet. Postmodern orthodoxy by definition must have undergone a deep immersion in modernity, worked for it, hoped with it, clung to it, and been thoroughly instructed by it, yet finally has turned away from it in disillusionment, only to come on classical Christianity as surprisingly more wise, realistic, resourceful, and creative than modernity itself.

The analogy is one of an estranged love affair. Premodern orthodoxy never fell in love with modernity or never came close enough to be enamored of it. Postmodern orthodoxy quite differently is on the rebound from a heavy, entangling affair that held out the most ecstatic promises but never delivered. If postmodern orthodoxy is a little gruff and cynical at times, it is because it has been burned by these broken promises. That is why it is *post.* It lives in the afterburn of lost idealisms.

Yet it is orthodox only in the most embryonic sense. It is only now beginning to discover a love more chaste and true. It is not in a cynical mood, except when it feels its old wounds, the deep aches and hurts that it knows only time will heal. And yet as a young lover it remains awkward and ungainly in the presence of its beloved. It is not yet a suave, confident, experienced lover.

In fact, it remains a serious question for premodern orthodoxy as to whether postmodern orthodoxy should even be called *orthodoxy* at all, for it has so much to learn, so far to go on the way to becoming well instructed. It has not learned its Greek and Latin well. Its garb, music, and vernacular make it still look far more like modernity than orthodoxy to those who see it only from the vantage point of premodern orthodoxy. But the postmoderns have had a rich series of experiences that premoderns have not had and are able to see Christian truth refracted through these experiences in a way that premoderns find impossible. Premoderns have never been dazzled by or yearned for modernity or become enmeshed in an involved engagement or snarled bond with it. They may have touched it artificially, but they were never engrossed in it or loyal to it. That is the mark of postmodern Christians. They have been in love, and shared modernity's dreams and hopes, only later to experience a restlessness that eventually finds its rest only in the mercy of God that modernity thinks it can do without.

In this sense, much of the self-proclaimed orthodoxy we see around us is out-and-out premodern. This is not to say it is bad, but only that it lacks deep immersion in modernity, for good or ill. How does postmodern orthodoxy look upon premodern orthodoxy? With admiration for its rigor, and sometimes with wistfulness that it had mastered disciplines now virtually lost, and yet with the awareness that premodern orthodoxy will not really do for the postmodern situation. Today we know full well that it is up to us to reappropriate the ancient tradition *in* the modern setting, and no one can do it for us. So however much we may admire the tradition maintenance of the Copts or Amish or the pre-Emancipation Judaism of the eighteenth-century stetel, none of these can serve as direct paradigms for the post modern renewal of the Jewish-Christian tradition, because they have so strictly barricaded themselves against all forms of alluring intercourse with modernity.

Not so with postmoderns, who have already roamed widely through and risked radical encounters with the therapies, sciences, philosophical methodologies, political strategies, and aspirations of modernity, yet have not found there the buried treasure that was advertised. They have plunged to the depths of psychoanalysis, behavior modification, structuralist sociology, relativity theory, and quantum physics, existential ethics, Marxist politics, and alleged sexual "liberations" of every kind, and yet have come away from modernity more demoralized, only belatedly to discover that the classical Jewish-Christian tradition is wiser and better, more realistic and humane.

Paul of Tarsus is an earlier prototype of the same pattern of one who first underwent the full rigors of a hellenizing Judaism, opposed Christianity with all his might, immersing himself completely in its opposition, only then later to emerge out of this experience as Christianity's most eloquent spokesmen to those least inclined otherwise to understand it. Orthodoxy has repeatedly learned that it is best defended and understood by those who have once known and later renounced false opinion. For it is precisely through attacking the faith that one comes to see it from the outside in a relation of special intensity and therefore is able to grasp it later from the inside with a special intensity. The true faith is articulated with best results, wrote Leo to Chalcedon, when heterodoxy is resisted by those who have understood it best by having had the direct experience of following the madness of apostasy, only later to perceive its inconsistency or pretense. By analogy, those who have most deeply shared in the illusions of modernity may be best prepared to understand the complexities and depth of modernity's challenge to Christianity. If psychoanalysis, for example, constitutes a substantial challenge to Christian anthropology, how can one respond realistically unless one has first empathized sufficiently with psychoanalysis to grasp its challenge, which is not easily perceived by premodern consciousness?

In addition to my young students, most of them born after 1950, my personal mentors in this journey have been a few characters seemingly born out of time—I mention particularly Will Herberg, Edwin Lewis, Joseph Mathews, and Albert Outler. For they all participated deeply, vigorously, and with life-involving commitments in radical politics and liberal hopes (Herberg with the Communist Party, Lewis with the social gospel, Mathews with existentialism, and Outler with reductive naturalism); only later, having experienced the exaggerated promises and pretensions of modernity, did they turn to the pit from whence they were digged. Among earlier prototypes who anticipated postmodern orthodoxy in profound ways I owe unending debts to J. H. Newman, Søren Kierkegaard, G.K. Chesterton, C. S. Lewis, and T. S. Eliot. But none of these can be said to be truly postmodern except in a highly provisional and anticipatory sense, because modernity had not yet played out its spectacular disintegration in their lifetimes.

Neo-Orthodoxy: Why Did It Fail?

An understandable confusion that arises among some sophisticated audiences is the assumption that we are really thinking of the neo-orthodoxy of Karl Barth and Reinhold Niebuhr when we speak of postmodern orthodoxy. It is an understandable case of mistaken identity, and one that needs to be cleared up decisively. Neo-orthodoxy, by no fault of its own, did not live deep enough into the outrageous decline of the twentieth century to behold the precipitous moral deterioration of modernity. Barth and Paul Tillich in the 1920s could see the cracks in the surface, but it was not until the late 1960s and 1970s that the structural nature of those cracks became fully evident. All of the major exponents of neo-orthodoxy thought of themselves basically as reformist change agents rather than conservators of tradition, a spirit that runs directly counter both to pre- and postmodern orthodoxy. Whatever differences they might have had among them, all of them—from Emil Brunner to Anders Nygren, from Friedrich Gogarten to Rudolf Bultmann—thought of themselves as programmatic theologians, essentially out to alter the tradition rather than sustain, cultivate, and nurture it. Furthermore, neo-orthodoxy on the whole was enormously bored by liturgy, sacrament, pastoral care, and concrete tasks of ministry—all issues with which we are now deeply engrossed. Most major neo-orthodox figures (notably Tillich, Barth, and Niebuhr) have been greatly enamored at times with messianic socialist politics, a tempting habit that postmoderns, to the man or woman, have found it necessary to kick.

Suppose we take Reinhold Niebuhr as a leading prototype of neo-orthodoxy, as many do, despite the fact that he himself detested the term. How well does Niebuhr resonate with what we are calling *postmodern orthodoxy?* Not very well. For Niebuhr, it must be remembered, conducted an unrelenting polemical campaign against what he called *orthodoxy,* from his first book, *Does Civilization Need Religion?* to his last one, *Man's Nature and His Communities.* He consistently viewed himself under a reformist self-image as one who was battling to reverse the trend of a wayward classical tradition that had become inextricably mired in social inequities and bourgeois conservatism. Although postmodern students can learn a great deal from Niebuhr about the criticism of modernity, he would hardly have had much sympathy for their fascination with the sociology of tradition maintenance or for their Chalcedonian Christology or trinitarianism. Niebuhr had more confidence in the moral resources of the lone individual (note *Moral Man and Immoral Society*) than in the wisdom of the social process, on which orthodoxy hangs its theological method, and, although he was a critic of autonomous individualism, he never accurately estimated the depth of the gross interpersonal failures to which it was leading us.

If not Niebuhr, then suppose we take Barth as a prototype of neo-orthodoxy. Barth cannot be termed postmodern in our sense because he never entered empathically enough into the categories of modernity. To the degree that he is orthodox, he is more premodern or antimodern than postmodern. Although once a low-keyed Harnack liberal, he was never grossly infatuated with the dreams of modernity. Barth is one from whom we can still learn the most, but it is only by some stretch of the imagination that we could speak of him as postmodern in the radical sense.

If not Barth, then suppose we consider Bultmann as a type of neo-orthodoxy. But Bultmann, more than any recent theologian, has focused on the accommodation of Christian language to modern categories, particularly to the existentialism of Heidegger, hoping to demythologize the Christian message in order to gear it into categories "acceptable to the modern mind." So the energies of Bultmann's project are flowing precisely in the opposite direction from the spirit of postmodern orthodoxy. And one might say the same generally of Tillich, who made a massive attempt to correlate Christian categories to the cultural assumptions and existential questions of modernity. Thus all the major representatives of neo-orthodoxy fail to provide adequate models for postmodern orthodoxy, and it is best to not allow the two terms to be confused.

Without exception, the neo-orthodox theologians thought of themselves as radical Protestants standing in protest against both liberal theology and classical orthodoxy. Therefore, some decades later we sense a slightly adolescent psychological tinge or quality to much of their writing, attempting desperately to break free from parental inputs, both liberal and orthodox. Postmodern orthodoxy, on the contrary, is intently concerned to listen carefully to these parenting inputs from within the frame of reference of having passed seriously through and beyond modernity. Nothing is more important to genuine postmoderns than good parenting.

So there is a sense in which liberalism, neo-orthodoxy, and fundamentalism are all surprisingly more like each other than any of them are much like (either pre- or postmodern) orthodoxy in tone and spirit. For, although they all had different responses to modernity, they are all more deeply enmeshed in the spirit of modernity than postmoderns, who have learned by many difficult routes that modernity is only a fleeting stage of human consciousness on which Christianity must not bet all its chips.

Rather than confusing postmodern orthodoxy with *neo*-orthodoxy, it would be far more accurate to view it precisely in the opposite way, as imaginatively *paleo*-orthodox; for it seeks only to represent the *old* orthodoxy in a credible way amid the actual conditions of the modern world. It is searching for its premodern roots, yet joyfully living before God within the framework of modern pluralism. It is, in short, the very classical Christianity against which neo-orthodoxy constantly struggled and by which neo-orthodoxy was always frustrated and embarrassed.

Fundamentalism: Why Did It Never Try?

None of the people I am describing as postmodern orthodox are properly categorized as "fundamentalist." Yet whenever the term *orthodoxy* surfaces, some otherwise bright colleagues mentally translate it as a synonym for a fanatical, bigoted, Scopes Trial type of fundamentalism ("banging on the Bible and pouncing on proof texts," as one of my associates once caricatured it). So to avoid this misplaced identity, it is necessary to show precisely how the postmodern recovery of ancient ecumenical orthodoxy differs from recent Protestant fundamentalism.

In pursuing this distinction, I do not want to offend my evangelical or neoevangelical colleagues by cheaply and inaccurately pinning the older label of *fundamentalism* on those who have long ago disavowed it. I realize that the worst habits of fundamentalism have already been broken by most neoevangelical scholars, even though those improvements have hardly been well-recognized among liberal circles, who still prefer to wield the word *fundamentalism* as a polemical club or straw man. So it seems due time to identify the concept of fundamentalism historically with some accuracy in order to distinguish it from orthodoxy.

The five "fundamentals" of the Bible Conference at Niagara, 1895, offer a fascinating *selection* of doctrines as a nucleus for Christian thought: plenary inspiration of inerrant scriptures, the virgin birth, the substitutionary theory of atonement, the bodily resurrection of Jesus and the imminent second coming of Christ. If you reflect on it, the major premise of nineteenth-century historicism (that faith is based on historical facts and evidence) is much more determinative in the selection of these points than either patristic or Protestant scholastic orthodoxy. Why are these five concerns more "fundamental" than others, such as divine providence, justification by faith through grace, or the triune God? What is the principle of selection? Where is the church? The holy spirit? Sanctification? Sin? The principle of selection of these five fundamentals makes good sense only if seen in the context of nineteenth-century historicism, in which a determined effort was made to establish faith on the basis of objective historical evidence. Why was this so important when so little notice had been taken of it previously? Because the nineteenth century witnessed the powerful emergence of historical consciousness (Hegel, Darwin, Marx, Nietzsche, Spencer, and so on) that expressed a consuming interest in historical origins and evidence. Despite its protests, fundamentalism was inadvertently swept away by this modern historical consciousness and unwittingly became an instrument of it. It could not have happened in any century prior to the nineteenth. All this supports the arresting suggestion that modern fundamentalism is more akin to liberalism than either one of them would be willing to acknowledge, because both tacitly assumed that faith was based on historical evidence.

Carefully note the chief presupposition of the turn-of-the-century fundamentalist program subtly conditioning all its questions and answers: that Christianity is best defended by historically establishing its objective factual origin. This is the shared assumption of all nineteenth-century historicism. So it is not surprising that fundamentalism was far less interested in the doctrinal significance of the resurrection than the fact of the resurrection and did not defend the doctrinal meaning or confessional import of the virgin birth so much as the fact of the virgin birth. This is consistent with the essential credo of historicism that faith is based on factual historical evidence. In affirming this credo, liberal historicism and fundamentalist historicism remain to this day very much alike.

Although it may on superficial view seem that fundamentalism was simply not modern enough, from a larger perspective the more subtle problem is that it was too modern in a quite surprising sense; namely, that it was too deeply trapped in a defensive and collusive reaction to modern historicism, preoccupied as it was more with faith's evidence than with faith's substance.

So it is confusing when we persist in thinking of recent American fundamentalism as an ancient or time-honored view or as identical with classical Christianity. Even though fundamentalism belongs collusively to modern historicism, however, it still cannot be thought of as postmodern in our sense because it never became disillusioned with modernity, never risked a deep encounter with modernity's experimental edges, and never bottomed out on modernity's skid rows.

Those who have been involved in charismatic movements, either Catholic and Protestant, may wonder how the spirit we are describing as postmodern orthodoxy relates to their experience. The connection is this, as I see it: Those who have been powerfully moved by the Spirit are now being given an opportunity to learn more of the historical activity of the Spirit by which they are being moved. The Holy Spirit, after all, has a history. If charismatics focus only on the Spirit's present activity and forget the Spirit's past activity and future promise, they do not have a firm basis for discerning how the Spirit is moving in the present, or for discerning the difference between true and false doctrine. Not all charismatics are (or even wish to be) orthodox, nor are many of them postmodern in our sense. But many of the brightest and best of those whom we are describing as postmoderns have been reclaimed and reintroduced to the central vitalities of the Christian tradition by these energetic communities, at least enough to set their feet on the path toward deepened historical awareness, clearer doctrinal definition, and a fuller engagement in Christ's mission to the world.

Embryonic Profile

I have been trying to distinguish postmodern orthodoxy as an embryonic theological type from neo-orthodoxy, fundamentalism, from earlier confessional Protestant scholasticism and charismatic pietism. If it is none of these, strictly speaking, what is it? What does it amount to?

Some may in exasperation be tempted to say that all we are speaking of is the traditional Catholic *magisterium* wrestling with the deteriorating modern experience. Odd as it may sound, because this is written by and about and for Protestants largely, this definition is getting somewhat closer to descriptive accuracy, but even then it leaves much to be desired. For included within our definition of classical Christian orthodoxy are the Protestant theologies that adhered to the ecumenical patristic definitions. Although the thrust of this agenda will sound rather Catholic to free church Protestants, it will still sound extremely Protestant to most Roman Catholics. In any event, it seems fair to say that postmodern Protestants are digging deeply into the patristic and medieval texts that Roman Catholics and Eastern Orthodox have always found edifying. So be it. A rich stratum of ecumenism has suddenly been reached. And all this quite apart from the expected channels of institutional ecumenicity! The agenda for ecumenical theology consists in probing this deep stratum to discover what has happened to us, why our roots in the same early tradition are more fundamental than our differences, and why amid the challenges of modernity we need each other more than ever.

Who are these individuals we are calling the *postmodern orthodox?* Can we name any recognizable names? Although this would surely help the reader with the identification of a gestalt, it is more difficult than it sounds, because its best representatives are too young to have written significantly. And even the major writers they are reading, furthermore, often are not fully representative of the type. But it is easier to say who they are being influenced by than to present a cast of characters for a fully developed "school" at this stage. They obviously are much more drawn to historical than to contemporary figures. They are more likely to be found reading Cyprian, Jerome, Eusebius, or Ambrose than Harvey Cox, Sam Keen, Mary Daly, or John A.T. Robinson. But among contemporary writers, the social scientists that are more likely to attract them are Robert Nesbit, Philip Reiff, Robert Heilbronner, Lewis Feuer, Seymour Lipset, and Peter Berger. Among figures in psychology and pastoral care they may be found reading James Dittes, Don Browning, David Bakan, Thomas Szasz, Frank Lake, Paul Pruyser, Newton Maloney, and Paul Vitz. In constructive theology they will often resonate with Wolfhart Pannenberg, Helmut Theilicke, Yves Congar, and Helmut Gollwitzer, and among Americans writers like Avery Dulles, Herbert Richardson, Letty Russell, and Paul Jewitt. They may find certain public figures like Malcomb Muggeridge interesting, but are more likely to take seriously *Sojourners,* John Vincent, Jacques Ellul, or William Stringfellow in their more fundamental orientation to questions of ethics and contemporary self-understanding. Among biblical scholars, they will be found reading both European and American writers who wish to utilize but not idolatrize the historical-critical apparatus. Some are neoevangelicals, but just as many have come out a deep immersion in process theology; some are existentialists, others strongly antiexistentialist; some have come out of neo-orthodox backgrounds, others from Catholic tutelage; yet their views do not jibe closely with any of these movements. They tend to be independent and imaginatively self-controlled thinkers. They remain as yet small in number, and if they were all gathered together at an American Academy of Religion meeting they would seem no bigger than a distant cloud roughly the size of a person's hand.

4

Interlude: Candid Talk with Old Co-conspirators

CANDOR is an asset to conflicted communication. When I try to touch the essential energy and passion of this agenda, I envision a conversation not in a legislative hall but rather around a crackling fire with several good friends. The subject is "the future of theology," but at the moment we are deeply conflicted about it. There are five participants in this conversation besides me, all old friends gathered to reminisce about our salad days and battle scars. They include a hip Benedictine priest (Anthony); a social activist professional (Ted); a scholarly working pastor (Frank); Frank's twenty-four-year-old daughter (Jane), whom I've known since her pigtail stage and with whom I have marched and sung in the civil rights movement, who is seriously contemplating seminary education and ordination; and an evangelical black lay leader and adult teacher in an integrated church (Cassie). It would be too much to develop all viewpoints in the conversation, but I will try at least to state the essential viewpoint I would wish to develop in that long evening, salted with a bit of poetic license. I am not reporting an actual single conversation, but one that could have taken place; the names are not the names of real people. Keep in mind the premise: I know my partners well enough to pull no punches; I care about them very much, but at the moment we experience a wrenching and awkward conflict.

The Ironies of Catholic–Protestant Dialogue

Tony had been grinding on about Catholic charismatics, recalcitrant bishops, and his own inner struggle with celibacy, when I found myself saying, even to my own surprise, that I was only recently beginning to become aware of the loss we Protestants have sustained in post-Vatican II Catholicism, which we all cheered as we watched it unfold. I remember how moving it was to me personally to be sitting there in St. Peter's Basilica while the debate was was raging on *Gaudium et spes.* It softened my smugness, taught me how delicate the conciliar process can be, challenged my Protestant chauvinism and fired a wide-ranging new interest in ancient and modern Catholic consciousness. That was in 1965. Now, over a decade later, I am trying to assess the aftermath of Vatican II for Protestants. I am amazed at how quickly all of our worst Protestant habits have become Catholic addictions.

"You cannot imagine how much we have relied on you to be there checking our hairbrained experimentations," I told Tony. "We were free to do laboratory ecclesiology as long as you were there giving us a base out of which to be Protestants. After all, Protestantism began as a resounding protest, and you gave us something to protest against, and you have always *been there* for us—for four hundred years we could count on you with your canon law, priesthood, and sacraments. We have always had you to fight; but now you are less and less that impregnable bulwark that gave us a sure point of reference. Now that you have faded into what seems to us like semi-Protestants and tardy liberals, we are beginning to miss the solidity of your ('our') tradition. Probably neither of us has realized how unconsciously we have depended on each other for the mutual correction of our wildest exaggerations. The acquiescence of one pole of a tension that has lasted for four centuries has vast and unexpected meaning for the other pole. At one level, it makes us angry; at another level, anxious. For we are now going to be forced to carry part of that load you have always conscientiously carried for us. We are densely ill prepared. You are still well equipped for the task, but the only places we see you these days are where you are leching about after our favorite old Protestant strumpets—subjectivism, messianic idealism, emotive enthusiasm, and ethical relativism. You have abandoned us in the most seductive way by joining us!

"So there is a sense in which the developing Protestant agenda for theology today must be a very Catholic agenda, but no longer in the Vatican II sense—rather in the spirit of the counterreformation and Vatican I! For what was happening in the period from Loyola and Cano through Bellarmine and Suarez (I could feel Tony's blood pressure rising as I pronounced these names) to Vatican I? Essentially, an attempt to conserve and incorporate into the ancient tradition the challenge of nascent modernity and the critique of Protestantism.

It was characterized psychologically by a hunger for the delivered tradition and sociologically by institutional maintenance and doctrinal cohesion—exactly where the postmodern Protestant battle line now lies.

"But, when my closest Catholic confidants discover that I am thriving happily on the stockpiled resources of the very period of theology from which they are now trying desperately to escape, they are alarmed at my short-sightedness, and I am a bit embarrassed, because I do not mean to upset them. They become more vexed, however, when I show signs of uneasiness about the waves of reported new movements in Roman Catholic theology, movements familiar to anyone who knows beans about nineteenth-century Protestantism. I can understand, when I make an effort to be empathic, how they might be fascinated to discover a Feuerbach, a Rauschenbusch, or a Schleiermacher in new clothing, but I dread anticipating all the ills that lie ahead of them on those paths. I have had several recent conversations of this sort with ardent postconciliar Catholic colleagues who are eagerly reading Johannes Metz, Thomas Stransky, Ivan Illich, Hans Küng, Anthony Padavano, Charles Davis, and the rest. When I risk becoming self-revealing, I realize that what they are doing makes me vaguely sad, and I suspect that more Protestants than will admit it are beginning to feel the strange and unexplained sense of malaise about the rapid liberalization of Catholicism. Will Catholics be able in four decades to commit every major mistake that it took Protestant theology fully four centuries to make? The latest odds seem to favor it strongly."

Women and Excellence

Jane entered the conversation at this point with an astonishing analogy: "What you are feeling about Roman Catholic renewal, Tom, I am feeling about the women's movement today." I asked her to help me see the analogy.

"That requires telling my story," she said, "but I'll spare you the long version. I have plunged in, lobbied for, celebrated, and sweated over the women's movement for over ten years, since I read *The Feminine Mystique* as a teenager. Although I have always been a bit embarrassed by the brassy, outraged, frenetic edge of the movement, I am now feeling a deep sense of pathos about it. It's becoming ever more entrapped in the competitive, materialistic, bourgeois syndrome against which it earlier (validly) protested. I now feel a curious sadness that its idealisms, too, are being betrayed by self-interest and insensitivity. This betrayal is reflected in my own personal history. I bottomed out in the mid-1970s on a combination of consciousness raising, social outrage, assertiveness training, and "doing my own thing." I followed these with the Zen trip, the Psi trip and the est trip, only eventually to find my way back into my own Jewish-Christian tradition through the healing care and incredible love of a small group of genuine Christians whose lives were shaped by Acts 2:42, (sharing in the sacrament, praying, experiencing community and following the teaching of the apostles). Now I am trying to see my own trial-and-error experience in relation to God's grace."

Jane asked me what I thought might be in store for committed Christians seriously engaged in the women's movement. "I see Christian involvement in the women's movement in relation to its possibility—what it could be. Christianity is giving the women's movement so little of its depth. Only a tamed, faded, nineteenth-century religious optimism now stands in dialogue with it, and even that is becoming demoralized. I am searching today not for a way to discount or abandon the women's movement, but for a more complete fulfillment of it, enriched by a Christian understanding of love, human tragedy, and divine mercy. The movement urgently needs the wisdom of classical Christianity, but thus far traditional Christian reflection has failed to reach out for it deeply, allowing itself to be too much on the defensive. Only the Jewish-Christian understanding of sin can save the women's movement from its own self-deceptions, and place its already keen awareness of human alienation in the context of divine providence. Where do you sense the dialogue is moving?" "Keep in mind that I have literally grown up with the movement," said Jane, "motivated in part by my sense of Christian social conviction. The liberal Protestant concern for social justice brought me initially into the movement and sharpened my commitment to it (I was reading Betty Friedan and Simone de Beauvoir in a church youth conference at sixteen). I have been elated by its achievements and have despaired over its inconsistencies. It is no unmixed blessing. What frightens me most is its willingness to build a political movement essentially on *private* self-assertion, often to the neglect of community and covenant bonding. What began as a warm, mutual concern for group support tends now to stress purely *individual* self-interest. What is needed is an extension of the women's movement beyond its present urban and upper middle-class elitism toward a greater moral awareness, and above all toward the precious values of social continuity over which women have been the indispensable guardians. It is this potential extension of the women's movement that needs to stand in significant dialogue with

Jewish and Christian scripture and historical wisdom."

It was out of this autobiographical context that Jane addressed a poignant question to me: "To those of us who stand in this relation to the women's movement, it sometimes seems that we have no place to turn for wisdom in the dialogue between Christianity and equal rights advocacy. Are we expected to make it up as we go?"

"My first hunch is that you would do well to invest as much time with texts of classical theology as with the strident modern writers who assume they have transcended it. You know well the modern tradition of equal rights advocacy, from Elizabeth Cady Stanton to Simone de Beauvoir, Germaine Greer, Kate Millett, and Rosemary Ruether. You have already explored the heights and precipices of that mountain of literature. Now give tradition equal time. Let it say what it has to say to you in your post-modern situation. You need to get yourself out of the stifling trap of modernity, and I don't think you can do that by continuing to limit your significant reading to modern sources. Spend your best intellectual energies in solid exegesis of scripture, and with those historic church teachers whose passion was the proper grasping of the word of scripture (John Chrysostom, Augustine, Teresa of Avila, Calvin, and the seventeenth- and eighteenth-century Protestant divines). You need not be intimidated by the fact that most of these sources were written by men.

"If you are asking what we modern male theologians have to offer you, I am afraid that the honest answer is, 'Far too little'; we ourselves are not deeply enough rooted in scripture and tradition to meet the challenges we both face. The door is open for us to venture together. You might say we are on equal footing—equally ignorant of the scripture and tradition that could make us whole. In *Works of Love,* Kierkegaard wrote that the deepest level of our equality is our equality before God. His insight needs to be systematically pursued by both men and women, though men cannot achieve it for women, and women cannot bestow it upon men. The proper theological beginning for dialogue on equality is the radical equality of our dependence upon God, the misery that we equally share when we deny that dependence, and the mystery of our salvation from sin without preference to human status."

Affirming this context, Jane wondered if I had any encouraging word for women, such as she herself, who are considering ministry. "The irony of your struggle as a woman in ministry feels something like this to me: You will have to draw from the deepest spiritual wellsprings of the Jewish-Christian tradition in order to offset those distorted aspects of the tradition that have denied you equality and dignity as a person. This makes it even more imperative that you discover for yourself a rich depth of theological understanding of sin and salvation, judgment and grace, in order to overcome the plausible resistances in your own consciousness to an otherwise unjustifiable compromise with Christianity. You may find it exceedingly difficult to celebrate and enlarge the Christian tradition, while at the same time continuing to whittle away at the recalcitrant unjustices of the tradition. These conditions will require you to become more sensitive, sharper pastoral theologians than you otherwise might have been. This is precisely because you will have to discover plausible reasons resonating within the deeper recesses of the tradition to overcome the more obvious objections in your own consciousness to the inequities of the tradition as you know it. That is why I predict that an exceptionally high quality of of theological brilliance and pastoral awareness will emerge among women in ministry as we head toward the third Christian millennium.

"But at a deeper level my heart wrenches for you. It is a lonely pioneering venture on which you may be setting yourself. It is as though you were setting out on a long journey without any road maps. Who knows what will lie ahead? Surely you will feel the support of the community and your closest friends in crises, but when rejections abound, when alienations persist, when discrimination blocks your path, when others will not be able to understand you, will you be tough and courageous enough to persist and continue to grow through these adversities?

"There was a time, not long ago, when we could make pleasant promises to candidates for ministry for job security, minimum salaries, accoutrements, and splendid visions of upward mobility. Whether these expectations were a valid reflection of the essential tasks of ministry then is a debatable question, but in any event there is now grave doubt about how deliverable these promises may be in the future. What if very toublesome days should be ahead for the religious communities and for ministry? If the road ahead should turn out to be suffering, threats, possible imprisonment, and *marturia,* as I suspect some of it is likely to be, do we have a right to expect heroism and perseverance from women in ministry? Yes, of course we do; but it should not be entered into lightly or with flags waving or heady rhetoric, but rather with realism and prayer."

The Black Experience and Evangelical Christianity

Cassie wisely pointed to the wide differences between the black theologians holed up in universities and the black ministers whose theology is more powerfully shaped by a living community of worship. The black tradition of evangelical preaching, he argued, is a richer context for theology than the modern university. I agreed, and this gave me the opener to say something to Cassie I had been wanting to say for a long time.

"Right now you possess the precious gift of high moral credibility for your leadership and teaching. Use that gift wisely and prudently, without assuming that it will always be readily available. It is in part a legitimate white compensatory response for long-standing injustices, a psychological attempt to redress the grievances of centuries. But it is not to your interest to bet on its absolute durability. It can vanish in a moment, depending on the shifting interests of the partner in interaction. Beware of those who promise that everything you say counts double. If you play into that hopeless collusion, both parties will later have to pay for it twice over in frustration and disillusioned hopes.

"Part of the scandal of classical Christianity for you, as for Jane, is that it comes to you delivered by the very Western culture that has in fact been a source of vast oppression for you. There is in all Jewish and Christian experience a scandal of particularity, that God meets us through special histories that reveal larger dimensions of meaning in universal history. The theological irony of your black American Christian tradition is that the message of spiritual freedom in Jesus was transmitted to you through a culture that robbed freedom, plundered dignity, and scarred deeply. But as it has happened so many times before when the treasure (of the gospel) is carried in earthen vessels (wicked and unjust cultures), your black tradition was wonderfully able to sort out wheat from chaff. It remains on your theological agenda to make more sense of these deep ironies. In taking up that task, you are not alone. Other peoples, such as the Jews and Armenians, have faced genocidal threats, and many more have endured humiliating slavery for periods of time only later to recover their human dignity and historic identity, notably the Greeks, the Irish, and the Slavs. Your struggle to understand your history as Christians rightly should be seen alongside these other genocidally threatened histories of dispossessed peoples. Jesus himself came as a poor man from an enslaved nation. And it was his own brother James who pensively asked: 'Listen, my friends. Has not God chosen those who are poor in the eyes of the world to be rich in faith and to inherit the kingdom he has promised to those who love him?' (James 2:5)."

I tried to express to Cassie my hope that he would not be so mesmerized by the alluring ideologies of modernity that he forgot his own black history of alienation or failed to see it in the light of God's own suffering for us. "My prayer is that your suffering will be illumined by the suffering of Christ for you and will bestow significance on the suffering we all from time to time face and are called to meet courageously. A crucial effort in the emerging theological agenda must be a nonhedonistic pastoral theodicy that is learning to think theologically about and deal pastorally with those inevitable concomitants of human freedom: anxiety and guilt. If Kierkegaard was right, suffering and its meaning remains the central problem of religious consciousness. Christianity addresses a word to us about our suffering that transforms both our understanding of our suffering and the existing situation of our suffering, healing our wounds. Persons and groups who have more intensely experienced social and interpersonal alienation and who know suffering not merely as a concept but a daily grind are far better prepared to understand and proclaim the gospel of God's suffering love than are the self-satisfied hedonic types.

This is why the black Protestant tradition has been so rich in supplying vital energy to the white Protestant tradition. Black music has taught us to dance and sing the blues, but these teachings have not come without tears and suffering; rather, only by means of them. Black music, even in its secularized forms, has exceptional authenticity for us because we know intuitively that it has been hammered out of profound sufferings transmuted by faith. The moral credibility you now possess and to which our white liberal conscience gives assent, has been hard won. What I fear is that you might be easily outpromised by the immediatist messianic illusions of modernity so as to imagine that you can easily transcend by political rhetoric or psychological strategems the fundamental paradox and tension that characterize human existence."

I implored Cassie not to let himself get trapped in the role of a victim by allowing others to view him essentially as dependent and therefore as having lost his inner dignity and initiative. "This is far too much to grant, and if you do it you will spend most of your time in interactions trying to correct its imbalances, even though you may momentarily want to benefit from the generous, nurturant promises of the partner in the protector role."

The Working Pastor as Theologian

Meanwhile, Frank had been weaving in and out of these conversations, and, although his part will not be reported in detail, the gist of his concern throughout was the failure of academic theology to be of much help to the working pastor in his complex locus of responsibilities and crises. Frank, I might say, is a superb preacher, the kind whose preaching you benefit by hearing week by week because you know it corresponds with his existence as a person. What's more, he is a sensitive counselor and an astute spiritual leader of a fairly large urban congregation. In my view, he fulfills the teaching office of ministry in a magnificent way in his parish. So that made his question come to me with even more force. He essentially was asking me, "When are you and other theologians going to develop a theological understanding that I can translate meaningfully into my daily parish ministry?"

I answered with another question: "When are you going to show us how theological reasoning can emerge concretely out of your own actual experience of ministry?"

"We in academic theology must learn from you," I said to Frank. "We cannot any longer play the game of pretending that our highest duty is to import the next wave of theology from European universities or revolutionary political movements until finally it may filter down from the seminaries to the pastoral institutes and clergy retreats to the local pastor and congregation in some 'regrettably distorted form'. The flow must move exactly in the opposite direction, like a great tree drawing up nourishment and water from its roots. Only where the living tradition is being embodied by an actual community —only there is Christian teaching hale and hearty. It is only out of the matrix of a credible embodiment of Christian community that good theology can vitally emerge. That is the territory of the pastor. That is where the best theological intuitions of the coming decades will be formed. I have the hunch that the next move in theology may be up to you, Frank, and others like you, rather than we in the academic centers who have systematically forgotten how to think theologically out of a living community of worship and service, a lesson we might have been expected to have learned from a

Cyprian, a Calvin, a Wesley, or even a Schleiermacher.

"The neglect by academic theology of the essential subject matter of theology might be compared to the situation that would prevail if lawyers were to forget momentarily about trying cases in the courts and instead turn to the study of the literary analysis and esthetic critique of court opinions. When teaching ministers ignore the body of theology and church teaching in favor of other 'more relevant' disciplines and 'more interesting' bodies of knowledge, (often the silliest pop therapies and fad politics), the situation is comparable to law teachers who would ignore the history of case law or heart surgeons who would leave the hospital and become preoccupied instead with the heart as a symbol of inwardness. Just as lawyers belong in courts and surgeons in hospitals, so ministers belong in the gathered religious community, gathered in order to facilitate its scattering into the world with renewed spiritual understanding. Our tradition of jurisprudence is alive where evidence is being examined by due process, where juries are sorting out the facts, and where judges are determining which law shall apply. Similarly, the religious tradition is alive where the religious community is remembering and celebrating divine grace, where the word is fittingly preached and the sacraments fittingly received.

"Recently," I chided Frank, "I think you have been giving up on theology, largely because you perceive that theology has given up on you. Only a few years ago, you were reading theology avidly. How long has it been since you have carefully exegeted a scriptural text or read a classical theological treatise or worked deeply through a tough theological perplexity? My guess is that you have read two books on psychology for every theological book you have read in the past ten years. Why? One principal reason is that many theological writers have not been even slightly interested in really addressing your dilemmas, much less listening to you. They have been on a different upward mobility pattern, trying to gain credentials in the university community with colleagues who by and large think what you are doing is dull or naive. But you have also colluded with the faddists who have offered easy answers to the human dilemma by your granting them premature credence and not asking them the hard questions that come out of your daily ministry.

"Much of the history of theology has been dominated by the academic professionals in theology holding university positions, such as Abelard, Aquinas, Melanchthon, and Schleiermacher. But there have been several key periods of theological development when the pivotal insights have come from persons quietly engaged in daily ministry. This is particularly true of the first five centuries of the church's life, with great pastoral figures such as the Shepherd of Hermas, Polycarp, Irenaeus, and Ambrose, but it is also seen in the tradition of Richard Hooker, Philipp Jakob Spener, Richard Baxter, and John Wesley, and right into the modern period with such powerful figures as Walter Rauschenbusch, Reinhold Niebuhr, and Martin Luther King, Jr. What would the history of theology have done without these key persons doing their theological reflection directly out of their actual ministries? It strikes me that we are just in such a period today, where academic theology has played itself out or disavowed its task to such an extreme degree that perhaps the immediate future of theology literally depends on the imagination and insight of persons in daily 'ordinary ministries.'

"If we focus on the early centuries of the church's existence, we find it difficult to think of a single theological voice that was not in the pastoral office, either as a bishop or elder, serving in a teaching ministry and accountable to an actual pastoral setting. Today we erroneously assume that anyone who is pastor of a congregation or administrative leader of the church cannot possible have time to do decent theological work. But not so in the first half of the church's historical existence. During the first millennium, it would have been unthinkable for anyone to regard himself as a Christian theologian unless he were serving daily in the pastoral teaching office. In the early centuries, doctrinal definition was never done by 'professional' *non*pastoral theologians, but rather by practicing liturgists, preachers, and pastors engaged in the care of souls. Some correctives along this line are needed today."

The Moral Crisis of Social Activism

Alongside these conversations, another more volatile one had been brewing with my old social activist confrére Ted, who stands in the best tradition of William Lloyd Garrison, Rosemary Cady Stanton, A. J. Muste, the Berrigans, and Camilo Torres. He frankly expressed his horror at my fixation on suffering, my fascination with counter reformation Catholic thought and tradition maintenance, and the excessive confidence I am inclined to show toward the average pastor. He wondered if I have sold out completely on my commitment to a politically relevant theology. He himself is ordained but no longer maintains an active relation with his church judicatory. He inhabits a bureaucratic agency office in Manhattan that towers over the Hudson river, from which he can glimpse the huddled masses and the working poor. Although he despairs over all institutionalized religion, no one is more trapped in it professionally than he, who works daily as a liason between church agencies and government officials.

Ours is an old friendship that candor could never spoil. Having listened carefully to him unload on me, however, I felt that it was time for me to level with him about some of my long-held feelings of uneasiness about his inconsistencies and self-deceptions. This turned out to be the most painful exchange of the evening, because our comradeship goes back so far. But, hoping that our relationship might be tested in a different way and reconstructed on a better foundation, I confronted him with a long chain of questions, complaints, and grievances. These took on a momentum of their own and unfortunately become somewhat overstated, but they seemed contextually necessary in order to redefine where we were in our separate modes of consciousness. Even though they now seem excessively harsh, I think it is best to express them as frankly as I did that evening, in order to reveal the deeper emotive energy of this discussion as promised. My side of the conversation ran something as follows.

"How unconvincing is your talk of justice and poverty when you remain in your protected environment with guarded entry points and doormen who keep track of all intruders! There you sit with your executive washroom key, Yale Club identification, and travel budget, where you can talk a good game of oppression but you seldom meet the suffering poor or hear their voices or touch their hands or look into their faces. You have not shared in the lives of the oppressed except at a very safe distance. You live riskless in a comfortable house, so don't think of yourself as a martyr. You have benefited from an education that you call *liberal* but that remains prejudiced against every historical period except your own. Aren't you, after all, the one from whom we have heard so much talk about how our ideas must correspond with our actions and how any religious vision may be dismissed if it does not have instant pragmatic results? It is *you* from whom we have heard that talk, yet your own life is a silent protest against what you have been protesting.

"By now I feel that I know you pretty well. I have watched you inwardly delight in the death of the cherished values of your mother's and father's generation—their hopes, their investments, their institutions. Like watching a lead demolition ball swinging from a highly leveraged crane hitting the walls of stately old buildings, you have enjoyed watching the collapse of carefully constructed institutions, bridges, fortifications, customs, and patterns of behavior that have been centuries in the making. You have shrugged and winked as the ball hit the collonades, the old tapestries, the façades, and the support structures.

"You enlist the language of the prophets. And it is true that the God of Hosea, Isaiah, and James inspired you to a social conception of sin and justice, to ethical claims implicit in religious awareness, and to a vision of universal social reconciliation. You have blurred that vision, and the religious communities for which you are responsible are in deep trouble.

"While you have talked *Realpolitik,* Ted, you have apparently remained satisfied with passing resolutions and forgetting about them, and more so about those whose welfare your resolutions presume to protect. You have played the role of protector of the defenseless, yet haven't you made their lives a little the worse by overpromising and failing to deliver? You express grave concern over the environment and the economy, yet you burn boatloads of fuel in your two automobiles and airplane trips to convention centers where you imagine you are serving church and society by again revising organizational charts and tinkering with institutional machinery, often with the hidden interest of maintaining your own prestige and power.

"Face it, the church has probably declined as quickly under the brief period of our current leadership as it has under some of its most bungling leaders in its most disreputable periods of history. Can you name any historical period in which a generation inherited a religious community with more vitality and left it more demoralized? You have accommodated yourselves thoughtlessly to the spirit of modernity and imagined you were doing the church a grand service by forgetting its historic understandings. Wherever this accommodationist influence has been greatest, the religious communities have gotten most quickly in the worst shape. Yet you have not been able to listen to the complaint of your own conscience, because your therapist has been trying to help you feel less guilty. In fact, he has defined emotional health as the absence of guilt feelings of any kind, and your diluted theology has colluded disastrously by acquiescing to that definition. Incredible. It is hard to believe that such things can happen to such well-intentioned people, but it is just your assumption that your good intentions are inevitably reliable that has taken you furthest off course."

At that moment I received a deep look of recognition from Ted, born out of many shared experiences. Gently he said: "Tell me what you want. What are you asking of those of us who, as you yourself, have invested ourselves in a life-long search for a socially, politically relevant Christian ethic?" Instantly I felt that it was much easier to state my critique than to point toward a constructive way ahead for Ted, for others, or even for me. But aware that his question pierced to a deep center that could not be artfully dodged, I took a deep breath and tried to respond: "What I hope from you, as from myself, is not a cheap reduction of the tension between the Christian ethic and political repentance, but an increase of that tension. I am not looking for a quietism that would cynically give up on a Christian political ethic, but a more realistic political engagement rooted in an awareness of the depth of sin and grace. I am asking neither for a return to culture Protestantism or to simplistic biblicism, but to a deeper critique of modernity rooted in scripture's grasp of God's providence amid alienated human history. That means less self-deceptive idealism and more Christian realism, less elitism and more respect for ordinary people, fewer hurried baptisms of disguised self-interest and more disciplined love in search of a social policy."

Although I am reporting only one side of this conversation, because this is a "viewpoint" essay, you can well imagine that the conversation had another side and that it was not without its own merits. The two-way dialogue that ensued was able to correct some of the exaggerations of my own outburst, but the purpose of this report is merely to get at the central emotive energies underlying this discussion, and I think they are revealed as well in that rough-and-tumble eruption as anywhere.

That is the substance of what happened, as I experienced it and responded to it—a one-sided report that surely could have been expanded into a chapter five times this length if equal time were invoked. Ted, my oldest friend among the group, was particularly stung and hurt at the depth of my outrage. What is ahead for our friendship is yet to be determined, but I felt that it was a good sign when, as he left, he pensively put his hand on my shoulder, looked me straight in the eye, and said: "Old friend, you are like the airline pilot who, fed up with the noise and crush and movement of civilization, decided to enter a Trappist monastery for a life of silence. The first day he was inspired and elated. The second day he became somewhat uncomfortable. The third day he was going bananas. By the fourth day, he stood up in the refectory and addressed his brothers: 'Brothers, it is time that we talk over this dubious rule of silence.' When he was hushed indignantly, and finally carried away feet first, he shouted as he was tossed out by the main gate: 'Now is the time, if there ever was a time, to talk over and express ourselves fully about these damnable rules of silence!' "

Ted, knowing me longest and best, had spotted my weakness. "Does that mean that I am as impatient with myself as I am with others, that I have low a tolerance for follow through, or that I am probably not personally ready for the kind of theological effort that I am challenging others to tackle?"

"Take your pick." Ted winked.

"Thanks, Ted," I said, "I need some time to worry about that." But I knew instantly how right he was.

Since that memorable evening, these items may be duly reported: Jane did go on to seminary, where she is now experiencing a significant shift toward historical consciousness. Ted was offered an attractive government agency position, but turned it down in favor of a renewed commitment to his ordination. Frank now is being rumored as a leading candidate for the episcopacy, but in his latest letter indicated that he has still has not found his way into classical Christian pastoral teaching, and still has not been able to locate a copy of Gregory the Great's treatise on pastoral care. Cassie writes that his adult church school class is now studying Jeremiah with exceptional effect. And Anthony has just gotten married to a petite blond psychologist with whom he is now planning to start an experimental human potential growth center.

II

THE LIBERATION OF ORTHODOXY

THERE IS a quality of lightness, easiness, and in some sense blatant unseriousness that pervades classical Christianity's dialogue with modernity. The Christian intellect has no reason to be intimidated in the presence of later-stage modernity. Christianity has seen too many modern eras to be cowed by this one.

Christian freedom delights precisely in this world as the arena of God's providence. This age is the only one we have got. There can be no room for maudlin nostalgia. But the cloak of modernity should be worn lightly. It is not a tourniquet. There is no injunction against chuckling inwardly at the comic incongruities of modernity, yet no corollary need to lay on it a heavy blame trip.

Christian freedom is a quiet laughter, not the harsh laughter of a defensive apocalypticism that cannot distinguish a minor cultural crisis from the End of Days. It is a laughter rooted in unmerited grace and historical awareness that knows that it need not grovel before either the dogmas or the myopias of modernity.

This is what I prefer to call a "liberated orthodoxy": being freed, by historical perspective and by evangelical faith from the illusions of modernity and for a eucharistic existence. So our motto might be, if we are going to campaign for anything: "Freedom now for the tradition"! For Christianity has a right to be understood historically, as it has understood itself, even as every individual person has a right to some degree to be judged not merely in terms of his present momentary transgressions, but in terms of his larger lifelong intentionality and long-standing behavior patterns.

5

The Craft of Pastoral Guardianship

THE sociology of orthodoxy is such an intriguing subject that it amazes me that it has been so avidly avoided by sociologists. Jewish, Islamic, and Christian sociologists whose temperament or value commitments are already toward tradition maintenance have an exciting field of investigation awaiting them. It is virgin territory intellectually, because of the preoccupation of modern sociological research with social change and the corollary bias against social continuity. In this respect, sociologists might do well to begin by studying the maintenance of tradition within their own sociology profession and the degree to which an official sociological doctrine or the apparatus of sociological orthodoxy already exists within their own journals and societies.

The premise of the sociology of any orthodoxy (Islamic,

Skinnerian, Marxian, psychoanalytic, Jewish, Protestant, and so on) is this: If social processes are to achieve multigenerational continuity, they require legitimization and careful tradition-maintenance. Without any authorized definition of a movement's teaching, it cannot span the generations or even assess the validity of potential misinterpretations. A religious tradition dissipates rapidly if it cannot define itself in relation to its cultural alternatives. The attempt to provide clear, authoritative doctrinal definition in order to sustain the cohesive basis of the community is called *orthodoxy.* Although this process has been poorly understood sociologically, I suspect it exists in every human community that has intergenerational aspirations and certainly in all the great religious traditions.

The Sociology of Orthodoxy: How Is It Illumined by the Jewish Experience?

Where did we get the twisted misconception that orthodoxy is essentially a set of ideas rather than a living tradition of social experience? Our stereotype of orthodoxy is that of frozen dogma, rather than a warm continuity of human experience. Yet orthodoxies are best judged not merely by their doctrinal ideas but also by their social products, the quality of their communities, their ability to nurture a tradition through multigenerational challenges, the ways they have found to sing, dance, marry, and bury. They should be studied sociologically, not just theologically.

Yet, in a recent conversation with several outstanding sociologists, I asked them if they could think of a single definitive work on the sociology of orthodoxy, and they could not come up with any significant titles. I later made a bibliographical search myself to see if they were right, and to my amazement they were. There is a fair amount of talk about pattern maintenance, legitimization, authority, and social control, but virtually none strictly speaking on orthodoxy as a sociological type.

A New York museum recently presented an exhibit entitled "The Orthodox Experience," a powerful visual statement of the living social experience of Jewish orthodoxy. The focus properly was on the human experience, rather than merely on a set of abstract ideas. The exceptional delight expressed in this exhibit made me wonder why we have so neglected the social, experiential side of Christian orthodoxy while we have so overstressed an abstract view of doctrinal orthodoxy as if it could be wholly disconnected from a vibrant living community. In fact, there would be no orthodox ideas without an orthodox community that was lively enough to sustain itself intergenerationally.

The exhibit also made me feel a deep tinge of regret that we liberal Protestants have largely formed our Jewish associations with liberal, culturally accommodative Jews to the neglect of dialogue with conservative and orthodox Jews, thereby missing much of the tough sociological substance of the Jewish experience and contenting ourselves with learning about Judaism only through a thick quasi-Protestantized accommodative lens. Through this lens both the orthodox and the Hassidic Jew have appeared to us as a dated, slightly comic residue of a passing ghetto existence. But, through powerful writers such as Abraham Heschel, Eliezer Berkovitz, Emil Fackenheim, and Elie Wiesel, postmoderns are beginning to learn more of the depth and vitality of the orthodox Jewish experience and even to perceive it as a powerful sociological paradigm, not only for Jews but for Christians as well.

Orthodox Judaism understands itself to be the authentic

conveyor of the tradition that prevailed over virtually the entire Jewish community prior to the emancipation of the eighteenth century. Jewish orthodoxy has placed somewhat less emphasis than Christianity on precise consensual doctrinal definition, and relatively more on submission to the authority of *halakhah* (practice, custom, and oral laws supplementing Torah), but its sociological dynamics are quite similar to Christian orthodoxy, as we will show. For Jewish orthodoxy looked on any inordinate adjustment of the tradition to the spirit of the time as incompatible with the *halakhah.* It held that God's revealed will is the final norm of human behavior, not the cultural context in which the Jewish community might for the moment exist. So orthodox Jews have vigorously resisted ambitious and overweening programs of "reform" that were motivated essentially by an attempt to accommodate the religious community to enlightenment thinking. It was especially feared that Judaism would be made over into a wordy quasi-Protestant phenomenon of general, secular, modern, ethical consciousness that would amount to an abandonment of the tradition.

Among orthodox Jews, there is no thought of gaudily "updating" the Torah or adjusting it neatly to the spirit of the times, but only of seeking to clarify its meaning in the light of ever-changing historical situations. The thornier issue, which has preoccupied a good deal of debate among orthodox Jews, has been whether or to what degree those who cooperate with secular cultural movements can still be regarded as orthodox. This debate has continued into modern Israel, represented by two important stances within orthodox Judaism: the more strictly separationist Agudat Israel, who have frowned on many forms of secular learning, as distinguished from the Mizrachi, who hold to orthodox faith but are somewhat more sympathetic toward worldly culture. The overarching concern of all orthodox bodies, however, is the maintenance of distinctive Jewish identity within emerging and declining forms of environing cultural expression. The mark of orthodoxy has often been the willingness to forego certain privileges offered by the Emancipation and expanded by modernity in order to sustain that identity. The overriding fear, of course, is of the uncritical assimilation of Jews into modern consciousness.

Just as the theology of orthodoxy requires a concept of heterodoxy, so does the sociology of orthodoxy require the drawing of lines that imply social negation, nonlegitimacy, and corporate rejection. We can see both of these strata, theological and sociological, in orthodox Judaism.

First, on the theological level, we note that several terms were used in the Talmudic and rabbinic literature to refer to heresy or heterodoxy. The Talmudic *min* (heretic, sectarian) was one who denied Israel's chosenness, the oneness of God, or the authority of the rabbis. Another rabbinic term for heresy, *epiquros,* referred to anyone who negated rabbinic authority, turned from the commandments, and denied the Torah, or whose views were in general "free of restraint." Among views considered heretical by Maimonides were the denial of creation *ex nihilo,* the denial of prophesy, divine revelation, or God's incorporeality. Other authorities extended the term *epiquros* to include any demeaning of the office of the rabbis. Another term, *kopfer* (a freethinker or heretic) was used especially for those who delighted in pointing out supposed contradictions between scriptural texts. One was considered a *mumar* (one who changes" or "converts") even if he rejected only one commandment of the Torah. Along such lines was the distinction between orthodoxy and heterodoxy drawn in rabbinic Judaism.

Various forms of social control and group negation were developed to express sociologically the lines that were drawn theologically between orthodoxy and heterodoxy. The treatment of the *minim* by orthodox Jews ranged from not sharing meals to forms of banning and excommunication. In some times and places, heterodoxy was opposed by means of a ban prohibiting marriage or by denying burial rites. Meat slaughtered by a *min* was forbidden; scrolls transcribed by a *min* were barred from use. At times, the *minim* were kept out of the synagogue on the grounds that they would further divide the community of faith, jeopardize the inner stability of the community, and/or scandalize the Jewish community before the surrounding world.

The Jewish and Christian practice of excommunication goes back at least as far as the Pharisees, Essenes, and Dead Sea Covenanters, who physically separated from their fellowship those who violated their central tenets. Among sects at various times regarded by orthodox Judaism as heterodox were the Samaritans, the Shabbateans (under Shabbetai Zevi), the followers of Jacob Frank, some devotees of the Zohar, and the pantheistic tendencies of Spinoza. Moses Mendelssohn was chief among modern Jewish thinkers to argue that all attempts to restrict ideas are self-defeating and that mistaken notions can be opposed only by gentle reason, not coercive actions resulting in separation.

What is post modern Christian theology learning from Jewish orthodoxy? It is more the learning of a style than a content and in many ways more a sociological than a theological learning. It is the discovery of an unapologetic pride and candor about being faithful guardians of religious tradition precisely amid the conditions of modernity without asking either for modernity's blessing or opinion. It is a willingness to fight and, if necessary, die for the continuity and authenticity of the tradition. It is the joy of dancing with a great historical community that has a long memory of God's mercy. It is being willing to be instructed by Torah and not assuming that we are instantly wiser on the basis of our limited, subjective, personal experience. Young Christians who are just beginning to venture into the postmodern consciousness with roots in antiquity are learning quickly and profoundly from young Jews who at this point in history have a deeper intuitive sense of what that means.

Is the Question of Heresy Askable?

The leading candidate for "most ugly issue in theology today" is doubtless heresy. We avoid it like bubonic plague. If we saw someone coming down the street whom we even vaguely suspected might raise the subject of heresy with us, we would find some way of ducking into a hidden place until he had passed.

Why? Because we are programmed to affable religious permissiveness and the rhetoric of compliance. Our least favored interaction pattern as Christian teachers is the role of a harsh judge. We detest judging, unless we happen to be risklessly judging something that is universally condemned by modernity. This is one reason we are not so swift at theology. Few of late have shown the courage to draw even the most elementary distinctions between the truth of the Christian faith and that which differs from it. We know that every affirmation requires the negation of its opposite, so, because we do not want to be caught negating anything, we do not make any affirmations either. I am exaggerating, of course, but the general pattern is a deep malaise in Christian theology, which hungers inordinately for the amiable reputation of "hail fellow well met."

The very word *heresy* turns our minds instantly to terrorizing images of the inquisitions of the sixteenth century and divisive heresy trials of later Protestant sectarianism. Even when we read the careful, closely-reasoned anathemas against heresy in the fourth century, we still cannot get the medieval witchhunts out of our minds. The sad history of the subsequent abuses of so-called orthodoxies have created grave obstacles of conscience for us today as we seek even minimally to understand the theological energy that went into precise doctrinal definition in the early Christian period. We tend to see the question of heresy only through modern lenses that fixate on the abuses of medieval and counterreformation political authority and thereby distort our perception of the intricate mosaic of earlier Christian doctrinal definition.

Sometimes the sobering history of repressions against heresy makes us wonder if the church's legitimate struggle to define itself over against what it is not (that is the essential difference between orthodoxy and heresy) has been intrinsically prone to destructive pride and overcompensation. The effect of the Hundred Years War and the period of severe persecution both by and against Protestants has made heresy a dreaded term among dissenting parties ever since the sixteenth century. The civil abuses against heretics remain heavy on the conscience of both Catholics and Protestants. So anyone who risks digging up the thorny question of heresy must be willing to learn from the chequered history of its abuse. To make good on this commitment, Christians today must be willing to work as hard as anyone to preserve political toleration for unpopular religious views. We can best do penance for a witchhunting history by offering vigorous protection to those threatened by contemporary witchhunters.

The emotional inflammability of the question of heresy might be calmed by an unhurried reflection on the ancient meaning of the term. Originally, *hairesis* meant simply a "different choice," an attachment to some teaching "other than" the delivered tradition, with some consequent disruption of the church's unity and continuity. This is why *hairesis* in the New Testament is so often associated with a divisive party spirit, a disruptive factionalism that was willing callously to strike out at the always vulnerable cohesiveness of the church. It was in its struggle to conserve the delivered tradition and defend it from challenges that the early church found it necessary to develop duly accredited channels for the teaching authority of the church as expressed through the office of ministry. From its inception, the office of ministry has been charged with guardianship of the authenticity of the apostolic witness within its limited, local sphere of responsibility. The *hairesis* against which it was charged to defend the church was not just any miscellaneous opinion, but rather any *heteran pistin,* any contravening faith or any opinion contrary to the apostolic teaching.

When Paul learned that the Galatians were quickly turning away to a "different gospel" *(heteron euaggelion)* than the mercy of Christ, he wrote them that there is no other gospel than "that which you received" (Gal. 1:9, RSV). "Even if we, or an angel from heaven, should preach to you a gospel contrary to that which we preached to you, let him be accursed" (Gal. 1:8, RSV). The authenticity of Paul's message was not, in his view, to be judged even by his personal presence, but solely by whether it was true to the standard of the apostolic teaching (1 Cor. 15:1–3). He exhorted his readers in Rome to "keep your eye on those who stir up quarrels and lead others astray, contrary to the teaching you received" (Rom. 16:17). The awareness of heresy that we find early in Paul we find expanded many times in later New Testament sources. So to imagine heresy essentially as a post-New Testament problem is a gross misconception. We have never had a church that had no difficulties with heresy, in the sense of struggling with challenging alternatives to the delivered tradition. In fact, a good case can be made that all the current heresies are essentially reformulations of the early ones familiar to the ancient church.

Paul argued that there is a hidden, provident reason why heresy exists so persistently among Christian communities: namely, "dissensions are necessary if only to show which of your members are sound" (1 Cor. 11:19). Heresy is permitted by the grace of God in order that the true faith may be reflected in the light of its inauthentic counterparts. Heresy does not just involve personal doubt or denial; it also must be understood sociologically, as a challenge to the unity and continuity of the church. Among the "deeds of the flesh" that Paul associated with the heretical spirit were "quarrels, a contentious temper, envy, fits of rage, selfish ambitions, dissensions, party intrigues" (Gal. 5:20).

Heresy has usually been thought of not as a challenge from some source outside the church, but from within it, in which some dimension of Christian truth is overemphasized to the neglect of the balance and wholeness found in the delivered tradition. So Ebionism was an overcompensated attempt to conserve the humanity of Jesus at the expense of his divinity, and Docetism was an excessive attempt in the other direction to stress his divine origin at the expense of neglecting his humanity and actual suffering.

Some readers of recent theology have come routinely to

expect theology to be looking for "something different" all the time. They have an insatiable hunger for "alternative approaches," "new visions," and "radical departures" in theology. These terms come very close to being a rough translation of what the church fathers called *heterodoxy.* Canon VII of the Council of Ephesus provided that it is canonically unlawful "to compose a different *(heteran)* faith as a rival to that established by the holy Fathers assembled with the Holy Spirit in Nicaea." Chalcedon defined that no one shall be allowed to "bring forward a different faith" *(heteran pistin)* or a "different creed" *(heteron symbolon).* The intent of the council fathers was not to prohibit the enlargement of our understanding of the faith, but only the production of teachings contrary to the faith once delivered to the saints. One of the commonest definitions of heresy in the early church was "that which we have invented" in contrast to "that which we have received." Yet the mainstream of recent theology persists in thinking of its fundamental task as that of doctrinal innovation, modernization and supposed improvement on the embarrassingly "dated" faith of our fathers. It is to all who hold this opinion that this minority report is respectfully addressed.

The Faith Once Delivered

It seems obvious to the average churchman that there is a solemn pastoral duty to conserve correct Christian doctrine, that the unifying center of the tradition is evident, and outrageous denials of Christian truth should not be permitted in alleged Christian teaching. So what is the fuss about, and what is the point of making an agenda item for something everyone already knows?

The problem is that this pastoral duty has not been vigorously pursued, nor the unifying center well identified. The ancient heresies flourish in every quarter unrecognized as such, often baptized and blessed by the parson's affable smile. After all, who needs controversy; and don't forget, the membership rolls could easily suffer from probing such questions.

Many liberal churchmen have a knee-jerk negative reaction to all talk of God's will, revelation, providence, trinity, not to mention atonement, redemption and divine judgment. Some look with contempt on most institutional Christianity, seldom participate in its eucharist, yet feel that they can with complete adequacy evaluate Christian doctrine and even stand as fully accredited teachers of Christian religion (at which time they present their degree credential from "a major modern university"). I am not describing a situation that does not exist. Unfortunately, it exists virtually unchecked by any rational criticism or caveats except those coming from the right tip of the right wing. It exists because our own liberal tradition has been sloppy in housekeeping and in reasonably monitoring its own criteria for ordination and teaching. Meanwhile, the faithful laity have assumed that the teaching office would be properly secured and accountable to the original message of Christianity. They have relied on their ordained ministry. As one who has spent his professional life in schools that educate ordained ministers, I cannot in good conscience say that the faith and hope of the laity in the teaching office has on the whole always been justified. That, if true, should be a special burden of conscience on all of us who share the teaching office. It is our responsibility to guarantee our own professional standards no less than physicians or lawyers, and when we fail to speak out against evident abuses the whole body suffers.

If we care about the authenticity and clarity of the church's teaching, can we remain passive in the face of out-and-out heterodox challenges to faith when they appear in our own specific sphere of responsibility and masquerade as authentic Christian teaching? Every pastor has to make situational judgments about when and where to attempt a response to heretical teaching as it emerges, but few pastors of conscience do not struggle with this problem in some profound way. What worries me is that theology of late has provided very little assistance in this practical struggle to maintain the genuineness of Christian teaching in the local setting. Is it so scandalous that we might hope that ordained ministers would represent the apostolic teaching accurately or that lay Christian teachers should receive competent instruction in Christian doctrine? One might think such questions would be answered routinely, but the fact is that they contain volatile issues that do not admit of easy settlement.

This places us unexpectedly on the creative edge of the ecumenical movement today, regrettably mired in demoralization and identity confusion. The unity of the body of Christ exists already in Christ, but we manifest it miserably in our institutional structures. It may be that the enriching of the church's unity in our time will occur only at the stiff cost of a certain purification of the church's teaching. We have brushed under our ecumenical rugs so many ancient heresies that our rugs now bulge in the middle. You may protest that the facing of questions so volatile as heresy will be divisive and thus will create in the now tranquil churches the very disruption that we associate with heresy itself. My experience in working with adult Christian lay persons leads me to believe that what they want and expect most from their ordained ministry is that it will deliver to them genuine Christian teaching and be able to distinguish it from the counterfeits. The risk of divisiveness is a necessary risk worth taking. If the term *purification* is too scary, could we at least agree that advocacy of classical Christian teaching within the framework of the open pursuit of the truth must remain a possibility within every Christian congregation and institution? Does that sound like an easy agreement? Don't bet on it.

Quality Control: Who Is in Charge?

The most avoided issue of contemporary theological controversy has been *haeresis.* It is precisely because it is so tempting to ignore it that it is all the more necessary for the emerging generation to face up to it.

The judicatories and bishops often seem unwilling or unable to oversee doctrinal teaching in their own areas or dioceses. Superintendents of ministers and judicatory officials often do not exercise any effective control over the quality of Christian teaching in their areas (I have made cautious inquiries among several denominations). Businesses have quality control on their products, but in Christian teaching, important as it is, there seems to be little quality control. Some, of course, prefer that it should remain minimal.

Those who look to the seminaries for theological quality control indeed have a right to expect it, but they should look realistically at the sociology of professionalization in theology today before they expect a quick turnaround. There are good reasons to doubt whether the seminaries with their present predilections are even prepared to grasp, much less solidly pursue, the problem. If not the seminaries or regional judicatories, then who is minding the store? The task will fall, as usual, mainly on the working pastor.

The Christian community has always been aware that God has providentially cared for its continuity in dangerous environments. Theology does not approach the future of its subject matter with grave anxiety or despair. It is not up to us finally to guarantee the continuity of the tradition, except in our own small and specific range of responsibility; but within that range it is up to us, especially among those who hold the teaching office.

For the faith to be delivered to each new cultural setting, each succeeding generation must come to grips with the original apostolic witness. Substitutes and glossy reinterpretations won't do. When we fail in our generation, we make it ever so much more difficult for the immediately succeeding generation. But, if it is elementary to the very definition of the church that it exists in time, it therefore must be a tradition and thus must understand itself as an intergenerational process. There is no easy way to accomplish once for all, on behalf of every generation, the task of the church, any more than there is a way for Judaism to accomplish its task in a single generation or to divest itself of the burden of tradition maintenance.

We have learned in modernity to keep fashionably silent about the atonement and resurrection and to develop theological positions less controversial and more agreeable with the assumptions of modernity—that Jesus is a good teacher (with minimal "mythological" additions), that God is good, but would not dare to judge our iniquities, and so on. In only one century of focusing on the ethical relevance of Jesus' teaching, we have almost forgotten how to speak of and pray to Jesus Christ, the Son of God and Savior of the world. In the well-intentioned attempt to deliver the Christian message in a language acceptable to moderns, we have peeled the onion down to nothing. We have cheated our young people out of the hard but necessary Christian word about human sin and divine redemption.

This has put us in a self-alienated situation. When we divorce Christian morality from its ground in divine grace, Christianity becomes a pathetic, almost laughable example of this religious contradiction: a highly intensified idealism that systematically cuts itself off from the energy that would make possible the fulfillment of that idealism. The power of the Christian life is rooted in the love of God who becomes flesh in Jesus Christ, without whom the radical ideals of the Christian life only tend to make us only more guilty and miserable.

Christianity has always been challenged to respond to hostile disputants from without. But the political regimes and tyrannies of mind and spirit from without have often been more manageable than the disavowal of faith from within its own household, enunciated in high-sounding terms by those who understand themselves to be doing it a huge favor. So it is not surprising that, from the pastoral epistles to the eighteenth century, careful attention was given to guaranteeing the authenticity of the teaching office of the church.

"No other foundation can any one lay," wrote Paul to the disputatious Corinthians, "than that which is laid, which is Jesus Christ" (1 Cor. 3:11, RSV). The foundation, strictly speaking, is not just scripture or tradition, but Jesus Christ himself, who is the heart of scripture and tradition, and whose mission to many generations requires both canonical scripture and diligent tradition maintenance.

At What Point Do the Remedies for Heterodoxy Become More Hazardous Than Heterodoxy Itself?

All our historical experience argues against the divisive, judgmental format of the heresy trial. It intensifies animosity and further polarizes positions that might otherwise be reconcilable through persuasion and dialogue. It divides the body of Christ. The circus atmosphere tends less toward procedural fairness than toward self-righteousness, harshness, and embitterment. So I say, "It isn't so," to the anxious thought that the trend of our argument might wind up in a recurrent round of ecclesiastical trials.

Anyone who launches out in the hazardous territory of our subject matter (learning to draw the boundary between heterodoxy and orthodoxy) should recognize a self-defeating psychological dynamic that accompanies the format of the ecclesiastical trial: Everyone loses. The victor in the conflict often comes off looking either like a tyrant or a malcontent. The loser gets the juicy role of innocent victim. The adversary situation is made for journalistic voyeurism, which is always happier to advertise scandal than take note of consensual achievement. The more outrageous the views under discussion, the more the media interest will gain sharp focus.

The preferred alternative to a coercive, adversary format is the ancient tradition of pastoral admonition and confidential spiritual counsel. This pattern is already well established in the New Testament, which centers far more attention on the gentle admonition of false teachers than on the courtroom paradigm. The corrective concern is focused less on laypersons than on teachers and less on coercion than on persuasion. Similarly, today, where flagrant heterodox teaching repeatedly occurs among those who have solemnly received the credentials and commission of ordination by a duly authorized church body that has approved their competence to teach Christian doctrine, the remedy of that body rightly will begin with gentle pastoral admonition, coupled with a clear theological rationale for the interests of the community in the authenticity of Christian teaching.

Is it too much to ask or hope that some judicatories or bishops or credentials committees or boards of ministry will have the courage on occasion to inquire about alleged flagrant abuses of the teaching office? Or, on serious and fair examination, if the fulmination against Christian doctrine should continue, would it not then be reasonable for a judicatory to ask the teacher to show cause why the credential should be continued, or how the person might properly be supervised or pastorally advised in the interest of the Christian community? Such questions open a Pandora's box.

Pastoral admonition does well to proceed with scrupulous concern for due process, fairness and the protection of the legitimate rights of all. "But," you may ask, "at what point does pastoral admonition constitute an infringement of civil rights or academic freedom?" Keep in mind that ordination is not a civil right; it is an ecclesiastical office solemnly covenanted to preach the word faithfully. The question of whether one is fulfilling one's obligation to church teaching is indeed a contractual question, but its adjudication lies strictly within the realm of ecclesial, not civil, judgment; for no civil law can decide what is correct religious teaching. That is quite beyond the competence of civil authority. On the same grounds, there can and must be no punishment for heterodox teaching other than simply withholding of the religious body's approval or permission to preach. That cannot be an offence against a civil right, because the ordination to preach is not a civil right. If in some future time a court should overextend its authority so as to dictate to a religious body how it is to monitor the authenticity of its own teaching, that would be a clear violation of religious liberty and should be resolutely resisted by civil rights advocates.

Polemics and Irenics: Neglected Frontier Disciplines?

In a heated debate with some of my colleagues, I testily suggested that what today's seminary most needs is a polemicist, trained in the rough-and-tumble give and take of old-fashioned scholastic Protestant polemics. They chided me patiently and challenged me to write an advertisement for the *Chronicle of Higher Education* that might attract a good polemicist; so I did:

> HELP WANTED: Christian polemicist. Ph.D. Must be courageous, honest, and thoroughly schooled both in the exacting logic of orthodoxy and the sciences of modernity; intelligent, witty, committed, tough; hard as nails in public debate, but with a warm heart and human touch; must be able to sharpen with precision the fine theological distinctions that modern audiences find irritating and difficult to grasp, yet make them clear and as interesting to us as they have been for others. Must be morally incorruptible and willing to die for the cause. We are an equal opportunity employer.

The irony of such an announcement lies not in its content, but in the fact that it would be utterly unthinkable that any respected seminary would even consider actually placing such an ad or making a search for such a polemics-person.

Doctrinal definition is as essential to the task of theology as identifying a phony dollar bill is to the job of a bank teller. To define is to set a boundary (Latin *definire:* "to limit, mark out, set bounds"). Yet we have been trying to practice the art of theology while studiously avoiding the embarrassing business of setting any boundaries.

Keep in mind, however, that there can be no definition of anything without excluding from that definition that which is different from it. In fact, that is precisely the definition of definition. And so it is with doctrinal definition.

Polemics is that traditional branch of Christian theology, now having lain fallow for several decades, that has sought to identify the proper boundaries of Christian belief and to distinguish the apostolic teaching from its opposites and alternatives. It is a border-defining discipline. As the courts and realtors rely on a surveyor to say "Here is the boundary," so has systematic theology in the past relied on the polemicist to say, "Here marks the exact line that distinguishes authentic from counterfeit Christianity." Yet we in theology today have preferred to do a booming business in religious real estate without any surveyor at all.

Suppose one is trying scrupulously to determine whether a particularly volatile, independent Marxist national party is "genuinely Marxist" or not? Would not all claimants instantly appeal to the classical texts of Marxism in order to settle such a dispute? Wouldn't the authenticity or doctrinal orthodoxy of subsequent schismatic spinoffs of later Marxism reasonably be assessed in relation to what Marx himself and other early theorists had said, and not the other way around? But in recent theology we have turned this procedure on its head by assuming that "modern man" must self-evidently be the final and absolute arbiter of the authenticity of Christian doctrine, and if certain segments of the Council of Ephesus do not fit into our modern assumptions we feel perfectly justified in blue-lining them out of our fantasies about "genuine Christianity."

The sister discipline that once neatly complemented and toned down polemics was irenics, from the lovely Greek word for peaceful, *eirenikos.* While polemics tried to mark out the borders of Christianity, irenics talked about the conditions for peace within the borders. While polemics tries to identify the dissensus that existed between faith and unfaith, irenics looked for the deeper forms of consensus within the community of faith. Irenic theology is conciliatory, reconciling, and peace making within the boundaries of the delivered apostolic tradition. Melanchthon, Bucer, and Cranmer are sixteenth-century prototypes of irenic orthodoxy. Vincent of Lerins, Thomas Aquinas, and Nicolas of Cusa would represent the irenic spirit in the Catholic tradition. Modern irenics reached its apex in the nineteenth century with the great works of comparative symbolics by J.A. Möhler, Philipp Marheinecke, Ferdinand Kattenbusch, G.F. Oehler and Charles Briggs, but from there on it was all downhill. It quickly became lost in the shuffle of twentieth-century impulses toward token and surface ecumenism. Irenics now awaits rediscovery and redevelopment as an theological and historical discipline. Its guiding principle then and now remains the ancient formula of Rupertus Meldenius that became so widely quoted later by Protestants: *"In necessariis, unitas; in non necessariis, libertas; in utrisque, caritas"* ("in essentials unity, in nonessentials liberty, in all things charity").

Polemical orthodoxy without irenic orthodoxy is combative and overly aggressive; irenics without polemics is borderless and diffuse. A postmodern irenics will concern itself with the cohesive center of the tradition, while an alert, adept, creative, postmodern polemical orthodoxy will concern itself with the circumference and try carefully to monitor the boundaries. Each needs the other, and both are urgently needed today. But they are lost arts, and their recovery is a crucial agenda item for theology today.

6

The Center of a Wide Circumference

ADMITTEDLY, there is a touch of comic incongruity in the realization that after 2,000 years of debate we are still not sure what Christianity *is* and still have royal battles as to whether it is even definable. It was W. R. Matthews who quipped that it seems even "more difficult to discover what Christianity is than to believe it when it is discovered."

The opposite point is more persuasively made by Kierkegaard, however, in his parable of the $100,000 gift, that we understand all too well *what* Christianity is but rather have to take extreme measures to protect ourselves against its rigorous claims:

> Suppose that it was said in the New Testament—we can surely suppose it—that it is God's will that every man should have 100,000 dollars: Do you think there would be any question of a commen-

When we hear the language of orthodoxy echoing in our modern minds, we are sometimes tempted to say to ourselves that surely we could have stated it better than that! It appears antiquated, mythopoeic, and harsh at best, and at worst narrow immoral or presumptuous. In those moments it is difficult to find the historical empathy necessary to listen carefully to the earliest creeds and symbols speak from within their own nexus of historical challenges and with the particular linguistic and philosophical resources they had available to them? Yet when we begin nondefensively listening, we sense a tremendously creative process in orthodoxy's active engagement with the changing cultural challenges it has faced. It has moved imaginatively through and beyond gnosticism, the mystery religions, neo-Platonism, Manichaenism, stoicism, Aristotelianism, nominalism, and many other sociocultural languages, right on down to contemporary empiricism, existentialism, and process thought, transmuting each one of them along the way. But these changing valences do not in themselves constitute an explanation of the center that makes the varied tradition unified. The identification of that center is a major assignment of the agenda for theology today, of which this discussion can only be a preliminary anticipation.

My teacher, H. Richard Niebuhr, was fond of quoting F. D. Maurice that most of us are right in what we affirm and wrong in what we deny. This book has necessitated so many harsh denials and required such a combative spirit that one might assume that such a wise maxim had been long repudiated. But, because I believe it is true, it is now time for me to redress the legitimate grievance of the reader who might think I have only relentless negations to offer and no positive agenda. So this chapter is offered as a modest constructive initiative in the form of a proposal for debate. After all, an agenda does not in itself finally settle items—that is what happens in the parliamentary process itself—but rather only settles on the crucial issues to be discussed. So, even if I do not work fully through the issue of this chapter concerning whether the central continuity of the Christian tradition can be defined, I would at least hope to be convincing that this is the unavoidable theological issue we must thoroughly debate in the last quarter of the twentieth century.

The Vital Center

Obviously Christianity has undergone many cultural transformations, just as has Jewish consciousness. But where is the silver thread that runs through all these changes? We must ask with well-instructed historical awareness: What persistently underlies all these curious mutations in Christian consciousness? The answer to that question would be the core of the tradition, the cohesive pattern, the center of the circumference, that which makes the Christian tradition finally a single tradition, not merely a legion of independent, absorptive, cultural accommodations.

Surely there must be many ways, not just one single way, to articulate this center, because Christianity has passed through so many symbol systems and worldviews. Whenever Christianity seriously has approached a new cultural formation, however, it has always found itself decisively instructed by returning to the most primitive attempts of ancient ecumenical Christianity to define its center, and that has meant not only early Christian scripture, but early Christian doctrinal definitions and symbolic confessions, such as the Apostles and Nicene Creeds, which have become widely respected as perennially valuable approaches to the core.

It is an elementary point in logic that something can have unity only if it has variety. Unity is by definition a concord of related yet different parts. That which has no variety cannot be said to have any definite sort of unity. So it is with the Christian tradition, that it has transgenerational unity in Christ only because it has luxuriant varieties in history. It would be comic to speak solemly about some orthodox unity unless there were in fact a genuine variety of cultural expressions of orthodoxy. It is on the basis of this premise that we speak of still another variety of orthodoxy, namely, postmodern. A new tonal texture, a delicate new shade is forming from the same source of spectral light that has manifested itself otherwise in other times.

It was this question that initiated a shift in my consciousness: Might it be that it is *only* when we richly behold the vast historical varieties of the orthodox tradition that we are finally able to grasp something of the central thread running quietly through all its flux? It is something like a visual puzzle that one can only recognize through much looking, standing back, and turning the picture at an angle, seeing it finally as a simple gestalt precisely through its awesome complexities. This reminded me of a startling image from Kierkegaard's Quidam in *Stages on Life's Way:* "When an examining magistrate has perhaps been sitting for a long time reading documents, hearing testimony, confronting witnesses, exploring localities—just as he sits there in the chamber he suddenly sees something. It is not a man, a new witness, it is not the *corpus delicti,* it is a something, and he calls it 'the course of events.' As soon as he sees the course of events, he, the examiner, has all he wants."[2] Suppose it is precisely in looking intently *through* the profuse

[2] Søren Kierkegaard, *Stages on Life's Way*, trans. Walter Lowrie (Princeton, N.J.: Princeton University Press, 1940), p. 288.

varieties of Christian orthodoxy, that we can begin to grasp with simplicity what holds it all together. What follows is merely my own impression of this "course of events" that enables us to grasp the unifying vitality of the varied tradition.

The fact that the tradition keeps on trying to identify its center supports the primary intuition that some center is necessarily thought to exist. I do not want to put heavy emphasis, however, on what I personally would wish the center to be, or what I think, by current public opinion analysis, a majority or plurality of modern Christians might think it to be. Rather, it must be defined historically: To what has the tradition itself through its liturgy, pastoral care, and confessions persistently pointed as the center of its vitality? Stated in that way, the center of the tradition should not in principle be regarded as mysterious or ineffable, because Christian preaching and theology have constantly tried to point to and articulate it clearly, even with frail and mutable languages.

When we listen carefully to the tradition speak of itself, here is the primary pattern that expresses itself in the mosaic of Christian liturgies and texts: The center of the tradition is *life in Christ.* Christianity is distinctive as a religious faith in that it understands itself (both originally and in the present time) to be living as a continuing community through the living Christ.

Christianity is not unique in understanding itself to have been founded by a particular historical person, for Islam and Buddhism both share that feature. Its uniqueness instead lies in its particular relation to its founder. Mohammed exists in an entirely different relation to Islam than Jesus does to Christianity; so also Gautama is to Buddhism not at all the same as Jesus is to Christianity. Without diminishing the significance of these companion religions, it is important for us to grasp the difference: It is the resurrected presence of the living Lord that continues to be the sole basis of the present reality of the church. Jesus is not merely the one who founded the community and left it, but rather the one who is present to the community now and in each historical period as the vital essence of the church.

If the central contribution of Jesus to Christianity were his moral instruction or religious insight (as some forms of liberalism taught) or in his establishing of a sociologically visible religious community (as some sociologies of religion have defined his central importance), one could more easily speak of structural parallels between Christianity, Islam, and Buddhism. But Jesus' importance to the Christian community is misjudged if seen essentially on the level of his moral or religious teaching or organizational ability or metaphysical ideas or even, strictly speaking, his own past life. Rather, it focuses on his present life as vitalizing center of the community of faith. That is what is celebrated in Holy Communion: the crucified and resurrected Christ not as a projection of faith but as that to which faith exists as a response.

The authority of Christ is the sole basis on which all other ecclesiastic authority lies in classical Christianity. Scripture is authoritative essentially because it witnesses to Christ. But Christ is far more than an authority for the church. Much more —Christ is the reality of the church. It is his presence that makes it cohere. Where the living Christ is not present, there the church is not present, at least according to its classical reasoning about itself. Christianity never tires of reminding us of this. Christ is the way, the truth, the life, the light, the living word, the shepherd. Christ is misunderstood as merely the one who points the way. He *is* the way.

Interpersonal Encounter with the Living Christ

So what is the unifying center of the variegated traditions? The experienced presence of the risen Christ in the midst of the worshipping community. There is no Christian tradition without some form of interpersonal encounter with the living Christ, however variable that encounter may appear in the many languages, cultures, and world views of two Christian millennia. Christ remains perennially engaged in the life of the world now as in the first century: "I am with you always," Jesus said to his disciples, "to the end of time" (Matt. 28:20).

However different Augustine's language may be from Luther's, or Aquinas' from Schleiermacher's, or Nicaea's from Westminster's, they do not differ in the slightest on this central point: that Christianity owes its existence then and now to the continued presence of the person of Christ even amid the most drastic historical reversals.

Note the varied ways in which scripture points to this pivotal theme: "By baptism we were buried with him, and lay dead, in order that, as Christ was raised from the dead in the splendour of the Father, so also we might set our feet upon the new path of life" (Rom. 6:4); "If we died with him, we shall live with him" (2 Tim. 2:11); "Did we not feel our hearts on fire as he talked with us on the road and explained the scriptures to us?" (Luke 24:32); "Where two or three have met together in my name, I am there among them" (Matt. 18:20); "I have been crucified with Christ: the life I now live is not my life, but the life which Christ lives in me; and my present bodily life is lived by faith in the Son of God, who loved me and gave himself up for me" (Gal. 2:20); "Now you are Christ's body, and each of you a limb or organ of it" (1 Cor. 12:27); "Dwell in me, as I in you. No branch can bear fruit by itself, but only if it remains united with the vine" (John 15:4). Nothing is clearer in the New Testament than that Christ is personally present in the life of the believing community and that Christianity consists essentially in participating in the cross and resurrection of Jesus. Cross and resurrection are so intrinsically linked in scripture that it is better to think of them as a single, complex event rather than as separable events with separable meanings. The resurrection is God's "yes" to Christ's obedience "even unto death," and the atoning cross is the only context for grasping the significance of the Easter narratives.

At one point in his writings, Paul deliberately attempts to identify the core of the tradition he is passing on:

> "Now I would remind you, brethren, in what terms I preached to you the gospel, which you received, in which you stand, by which you are saved, if you hold it fast—unless you believed in vain. For I delivered to you as of first importance what I also received, that Christ died for our sins in accordance with the scriptures, that he was buried, that he was raised on the third day in accordance with the scriptures, and that he appeared to Cephas, then to the twelve. Then he appeared to more than five hundred brethren at one time, most of whom are still alive, though some have fallen asleep. Then he appeared to James, then to all the apostles. Last of all, as to one untimely born, he appeared also to me (1 Cor. 15:1–8, RSV).

The same theme is reworked repeatedly in the earliest documents of orthodoxy, from Ignatius and Justin Martyr to the Presbyters of Smyrna, who in 180 A.D. confessed, "We know the Son, suffering as he suffered, dying as he died, and risen on the third day, and abiding at the right hand of the Father, and coming to judge the living and the dead. And in saying this we say what has been handed down to us." The same theme echos all the way into the language of the Westminster Confession: "All saints that are united to Jesus Christ their head, by his Spirit and by faith, have fellowship with him in his graces, sufferings, death, resurrection, and glory, and being united to one another in love, they have communion in each other's gifts and graces."

Other great historical religions embody rich moral sensitivity and spiritual awareness. The Holy Spirit has worked powerfully through them. But Christianity is alone among religions in its promise of salvation from sin, guilt, and death through a relation of trust in God who becomes flesh in a living person who actually lived in history, died and was resurrected, and continues to live in the present as the vital energizer of the contemporary worshipping community. Christians everywhere of all sorts, times, languages, and cultural assumptions understand the death and resurrection of Christ to be of central significance for their own personal faith and destiny, and for the meaning of universal history. That indeed is what makes them Christians.

It is this pardoning event of cross and resurrection that is printed indelibly on the mind of the church as the crucial moment in history where we are met once for all by the redemptive God who suffers for us and delivers us from sin and death. The church's pearl of great price is its memory and present participation in the event of cross and resurrection. Those who are not grasped by this event as the decisive endtime disclosure of the meaning of human history remain, regrettably, on the outskirts of Christian awareness. Those who assert that something less than God has met us in Jesus are by that (Arian) assertion ruling themselves out of the central stream of Christian awareness, the baptism into which we have been baptized. Those who try to conceive of Christianity without cross and resurrection do so only by ignoring what Christians themselves have universally said about the ground of their faith and the source of their experience.

It is a sign of the overweening pride of modernity and a mark of the new barbarism that we in the twentieth century pretend to have earned the right to judge and amend what Christians have repeatedly said constitutes the center of their consciousness. This has come about only because we have supposed ourselves fully competent to creatively redesign the tradition and improve it with our "superior modern imagination and insight."

With few exceptions, the ancient ecumenical consensus held firmly through the first seventeen centuries of Christianity—until modernity. Then it began to fade, split, and shatter. When we limit our historical vision to modernity, there is vast confusion about where the Christian center lies. The hymns, scripture, and liturgy of ancient Christianity continue to echo as a lovely chord through the decades of modernity, but they are perceived as anachronisms. Like the stones of Easter Island, the symbols of ancient orthodoxy remain standing amid modernity, but as mute witnesses to the living center once vitally known and celebrated.

It is only when we correct the myopia of modernity with a larger historical consciousness that we begin to behold the living tradition intact, and this is done essentially as an act of historical imagination and empathy. If we bracket out modern Christianity, we find to our astonishment that we must travel far out to the periphery of the tradition into rejected esotericisms and heresies in order to find the ideosyncratic voices that today predominate and often pose as "authentic Christianity." Admittedly the views of the Gnostics, Manicheans, Arians, Pelagians, and Socinians had local hegemonies for brief periods of time, but they never came close to meeting the criterion of Vincent of Lerins for orthodoxy, that they were everywhere, by all and always, held fast as apostolic belief.

Resurrection

In order to grasp what the resurrection meant to the followers of Jesus, it is necessary to ask what the prevailing idea of general resurrection meant among Jews in the period preceding Jesus. Everyone in that context knew exactly what resurrection meant: The anticipated end of history. The general resurrection was precisely the event that was expected to happen at the end time. The dead would rise and be judged. It was in that frame of reference that a powerful hope emerged in the century prior to Jesus that the end time would occur soon and the will of God would be finally revealed. End time communities such as those on the Dead Sea were rigorously readying themselves for the final consummation of history, for the resurrection of the just and the unjust.

The underlying assumption was that the meaning of history would be fully known only at its end. If God makes himself known in history, then it is evident that we do not know the whole story until the end. So we do not learn the will of God merely by looking at a phase or part of the historical process, any more than by reading the middle chapter do we understand a novel, but only by its end. Just as the meaning of one's own personal history is not fully revealed as long as one is still living, (because something decisive might happen at some future date that would change substantially the meaning of one's present existence), so it seemed to Jewish prophetic consciousness that the meaning of history could finally be revealed only at its end. And what was to happened at the end? Resurrection. The dead would rise for final judgment.

Whatever it was that occurred after Jesus' crucifixion, one thing is absolutely clear: Whatever it was, it was *called* "resurrection." Of that there can be no doubt. All who were met by it called it the same thing. However unclear many things may be about these alleged meetings with Jesus after his death, there was a consensus in the community that whatever it was that people were experiencing, the correct term for it was *resurrection,* which essentially meant the expected event at the end time of judgment and redemption. This is merely a logical and linguistic point, but one of considerable importance: Suppose the general resurrection was Event Z. There was a general consensus prior to Jesus about what Event Z would look like and what would happen then. Jesus came, lived, and died, and after his death a series of occurrences took place that were clearly called and unanimously identified as Z.

The significance of this is awesome: The events surrounding Jesus' death were experienced as the fulfillment of history, the decisive event of the last days, or at the very least the clear and decisive anticipation of the final event of history that reveals God's will once for all. So even though history continued to occur after Jesus' died and rose again, there was a sense in which Christians understood themselves through their meeting with Jesus to be in touch with the end time, and therefore with the meaning of universal history! This empowered the early Christian community with incredible courage in the face of seemingly impossible obstacles and terrifying threats. Why? Because their trust was not in this broken world, but in the risen Christ present to them as they sat together "at the Lord's table" or faced the wild animals of the Roman coliseum.

Suppose the prophets were right, that God's will is revealed through historical events—yet God's will is *finally* knowable only at the conclusion of the drama of history. Theology would then be intent on trying to understand, if possible, the anticipated *end* of the process, beyond all our current historical alienations, finitude, blindness, and sin. The earliest church reasoned in this way: In Jesus' resurrection, the end is already present, in an anticipated sense, and thus the will of God is finally revealed. So to participate in Christ is already to share in the events of the last days. It all made reasonable sense, seen from within the assumptions of Jewish historical reasoning, transmuted by an encounter with the resurrected Jesus. We today must learn to think historically in the hebraic sense, if we are to make sense of this central proclamation of Christianity. Seen in this frame of reference, the resurrection is so decisive that the importance of all other theological issues pales beside it, because it focuses on nothing less than the final revelation of the will of God in history.

We are searching for the center of the wide circumference of Christian sociohistorical experience. What is the center? *Resurrection* = interpersonal meeting with the living Christ. Not resurrection as an idea or past event, but rather resurrection as a currently experienced interpersonal reality. This is why interpersonal meeting has been a central feature of Christian theology from its inception.

Something so decisive happened anticipatively for human history in the resurrection of Jesus that it does not and cannot fit into our ordinary categories of understanding. We cannot rule out the resurrection of Jesus simply on the grounds (as Troeltsch's law of analogy would require) that nothing much like this ever happened to us before (how could it!). The event of which Christianity speaks is, like much interpersonal meeting, an event without analogy.

The least plausible of all explanations of the resurrection was that it was generated out of the despairing imagination of the disciples, for that does not explain why they were willing to risk their lives for it. Nor does it account for one of the most characteristic literary features of the Easter narratives, the report that the beholders were utterly surprised by the appearance of the risen Lord. The "surprise" element of the Easter narratives is too recurrent to be considered an anomaly. It is not likely that one would report being surprised by something that one had previously projected. No. *Something* occurred in Jesus' resurrection. It is quite unconvincing to assume that it could have been nothing. Whatever it was, it was experienced as the "spiritual body" or resurrected body of Jesus, and understood as the final self-disclosure of God.

Classical Christianity is saturated with this language about resurrection—both Christ's and ours. When the apostles began to try to express what had happened to them, they did not begin with a system of metaphysics or ethical injunctions or scientific data, but rather with their experiential testimony of an interpersonal encounter with Christ that "made all things new" All other forms of knowing were seen in relation to their being known in this way by God.

Once that point is grasped, everything else in Christianity falls into place. Human encounter is seen in relation to the divine human encounter. Our participation in historical existence is understood as a *participatio Christi.* Pastoral care becomes an active sharing in the life of Christ. Preaching is the announcement of the coming of the risen Christ into ordinary human life. The eucharist is the presence of Christ experienced sacramentally as a corporate enactment. The moral life is grasped essentially as the sharing of the love of God in and for the world.

If so, then the center of Christian doctrine has always been and remains resurrection. More than a substantial part of theology's agenda today, there is a sense in which, properly understood, resurrection is the perennial agenda for theology.

Admittedly the term "liberation theology" has suffered from overexpectation and the rhetoric of messianic idealism, but there is at least one sense in which Christian believers of all ages have understood themselves as being liberated: freed by the risen Christ from the power of sin and death, liberated *for* the neighbor and *from* self-justifying defensiveness, liberated *by* God *to* the life of responsible freedom in the world. "If then the Son sets you free, you will indeed be free" (John 8:36). "You see, then, my brothers, we are no slave-woman's children; our mother is the free woman. Christ set us free, to be free men. Stand firm, then, and refuse to be tied to the yoke of slavery again" (Gal. 4:31–5:1). "The life-giving law of the Spirit has set you free from the law of sin and death" (Rom. 8:2). "Live as free men, yet without using your freedom as a pretext for evil; but live as servants of God" (1 Pet. 2:16, RSV).

Shall We Sin That Grace May Abound?

But—now we hesitate. We have moral reservations! If Christ forgives sin, isn't there an ethical embarrassment at the heart of Christianity? Does not unmerited grace invite gross irresponsibility? Does it not tempt us merely to follow our self-assertive interests and then point cheaply to God's patient, unconditional, ever-available forgiveness? Is not Christianity of this sort potentially the least moral of all religions, precisely *because* of forgiveness? The same basic query was thrown at Paul: "Are we to continue in sin that grace may abound?"

(Rom. 6:1, RSV). Paul's answer hinges on this penetrating analogy: You are dead in Christ—dead to the old, alive to the new, dead to sin, alive to grace. Why should you foolishly continue to live as if you were dead?

In seeking to answer this objection responsibly, classical Christianity has always had to stress not only that God in Christ offers pardon for our sins, but also provides a community of growth, a context for actualizing freedom from bondage to sin, a *koinonia* in which love can be nurtured and experienced. To the preaching of the pardoning verdict (of justification, what God does *for* us to right our fallen existence) must be added a concern for nurturing a process by which the believer is drawn increasingly into the life of faith, hope, and love (or in traditional terms, sanctification, which concerns what God does *in* us to bring us to the fulfillment of our human possibility, by grace working with our wills). The bare word of unconditional pardon would be scandalously immoral without a community concerned with the ever-deepening growth of persons toward maturity in Christ and deeper participation in God's mission of love for the world. Christianity hopes that both persons and social processes will in some measure be redeemed from sin in fact and not merely in principle.

Suppose a governor decides to render a formal pardon for a criminal. He signs the paper, and the act goes into effect. But that does not necessarily mean that the criminal will be remotivated toward responsible behavior. The pardon is not in itself a behavioral guarantee. Similarly, classical Christianity has concerned itself not merely with toothless talk of God's pardon, but more with a supportive community and a structure for moral development by which that pardon might become appropriated in the life of responsible love. This requires a nurturing environment, a eucharistic community, a context in which the pardoned person can come increasingly to live in Christ, not in name only, but also in deed and in truth. This growth itself is the work of God the Spirit, encouraging and inspiring our own spirits freely to respond. The same God who meets us in the pardoning event of the living Christ is at work in this community.

There is an ongoing debate among Christians as to whether this process of growth is ever fully completed or in principle even actualizable so long as we remain "in the flesh"; that is, entangled in alienated existence. Lutherans and Calvinists have generally doubted that perfect love is possible in this life, while Catholic, Greek Orthodox, Anglican, and Methodist traditions have tended to say that we cannot put arbitrary limits on the ability of God the Spirit to refashion our lives. In all these traditions, however, there is an underlying consensus that grace seeks to enable a life of radical responsiveness to the love of God. If we have received the love of God, we are called to love as we have been loved, forgive as we have been forgiven, be merciful to others even as God is merciful to us. Otherwise Christianity becomes cheap grace. If good works never flow as a fruit of faith, there remains some doubt about the genuineness of that faith. Not that we are saved by these good works—never. We are saved by grace alone. But we are being called to respond to that active grace with active good works, sharing the self-giving love of God in Christ with the neighbor. In this way, the body of Christ becomes manifested through our bodies. This mystery is beautifully stated in Ephesians 2:10 (RSV): "For we are [God's own] workmanship, created in Christ Jesus for good works."

7

The Expurgated Scripture

I RECOGNIZED in myself recently a fixed habit that many pastors must share. In a casual, straight read-through of the New Testament last summer, I suddenly became aware that I had been consistently neglecting a certain portion of the New Testament, seldom preaching on it, and never including it as a deliberate focus for my personal reflection and teaching. I speak of the Pastoral Epistles (1 and 2 Timothy and Titus) and the General or Catholic Epistles (James, 1 and 2 Peter, the letters of John, and Jude). When I tried to understand *why* these later writings had been given low priority in my thinking, it required a rehearsal of the major influences on my reading of the New Testament: Rudolf Bultmann, Ernst Käsemann, Günther Bornkamm, and others, all highly respected leaders in New Testament interpretation. What follows is an attempt to track down the reasons why this pivotal part of scripture has seemed relatively closed to modern consciousness and to suggest how it might be reopened.

This chapter asks: Can the Pastoral and General Epistles of the New Testament help us reset the agenda for theology? My answer will be developed in two phases: to show how and why these letters have been widely discounted by leading biblical scholars; and to suggest that these writings nonetheless provide a rich mine of insights directly relevant to the situation of Christian ministry within modernity. In broaching these questions, I intend to address the working pastor more than the professional exegete, but the line of argument also impinges on the way one might proceed to teach New Testament either in a church or academic setting.

The Pastoral and General Epistles

Two scholars in particular, Rudolf Bultmann and Ernst Käsemann, have shaped a skeptical attitude toward the later New Testament writings. Both are highly influential—so much so that it would be hard to cite any New Testament interpreters more widely respected since Albert Schweitzer. I am not suggesting that they generally agree, for Käsemann has frontally challenged the Bultmannians on many assumptions, but they do agree firmly on the main point at issue in this chapter: that the Pastoral and General Epistles on the whole represent a regrettable deterioration of the normative (Pauline) theology of the New Testament. I would prefer, however, to let them speak for themselves in establishing this point.

I approach Bultmann with sympathy and appreciation, since he more than anyone has helped make the New Testament come alive for me as a modern person. On the point at issue in this chapter, I feel that I must have unconsciously colluded with him, along with many others, in chipping away at the New Testament canon in a way that has resulted in significant theological and pastoral losses.

Bultmann's account of the later writings runs like this. By the time of the Pastoral Epistles, faith *(pistis)* had become little more than a defensive piety trying to make "a place for itself within the framework of bourgeois living."[1] He describes the Pastorals as a "faded Paulinism" in which faith had become reduced to the "worn-down meaning of 'Christianity,' 'Christian religion'," which signified little more than "right doctrine" or "orthodoxy" *(TNT 2,* 183). The letter of James is even more depressing to Bultmann, since it lacks "every shred of understanding" for the eschatological hope that had intensified the other earlier normative New Testament theologies. Regrettably, in James "the moralism of the synagogue-tradition has made its entry," and Bultmann thinks it is even possible that its author "took over a Jewish document and only lightly retouched it." Bultmann testily argues that 2 Peter, like James, never gets beyond "legalistic moralism," and he regards it as a major theological setback that Christ is seen as a "pattern" for the believer. Similarly, Jude is thought to be moralistic and overly concerned with "pure living" ethics (*TNT 2,* 163–69). In these later writings, according to Bultmann, "sinlessness has thereby become a task to be accomplished." "In no case is conversion understood as the radical transformation of the old man," and salvation is "reduced to an event—the death and resurrection of Jesus—the effect of which, when appropriated in baptism, is to cancel the sins of

[1] Rudolf Bultmann, *Theology of the New Testament, vol.* 1 (New York: Charles Scribner's Sons, 1955), p. 183. Subsequent references to this work will be indicated in the text by *TNT 1* or *TNT 2.*

the past" (*TNT* 2, 204–209). Bultmann bemoans as sad evidence of theological *deterioration* (!) the fact that in the Pastorals "the demand for good works is everywhere heard" (*TNT* 2, 211).

Käsemann intensified this polemic by disparaging the Pastoral Epistles as a "case study in narrow-mindedness." In his view, "the gospel is domesticated," "early Christian prophecy is greatly restricted," and the church is trapped in a mood of "introversion," seeking to achieve a "halo of legitimacy."[2] According to Käsemann, the Pastorals have stupidly misunderstood Paul's theology, have "levelled it out," while freedom has become a private affair, stuffily "churchified," and the focus has shifted to "the apostolic succession of the episcopal office," which, quips Käsemann, is "one of the many Christian fictions" (*JMF,* 97).

The General Epistles worry Käsemann even more. James' talk about "the perfect law, the law of liberty" (James 1:25, RSV) is viewed as nothing more than "pretty phrases," "ornaments," which smack of "slightly retouched Jewish traditions" (*JMF,* 86). Even worse, 2 Peter represents a "relapse of Christianity into Hellenistic dualism"; "its eschatology lacks any vestige of Christological orientation."[3] Phrases such as "Our Lord and Saviour" are viewed as impersonal "stereotypes" without spiritual power. In the post-Pauline writings, Jesus' "red-hot message" has been reduced "to room temperature," characterized by "admonitions to live a godly life in quietness

[2] Ernst Käsemann, *Jesus Means Freedom* (Philadelphia: Fortress Press, 1969), pp. 88-97. Subsequent references to this work will be indicated in the text by *JMF.*

[3] Ernst Käsemann, *Essays on New Testament Themes* (London: SCM Press, 1964), pp. 178-80. Subsequent references to this work will be indicated in the text by *Essays*.

and integrity . . . combined intolerably with the political maxim that calmness is the citizen's first duty" (*JMF,* 87).

By the time the Pastoral and General Epistles were written, "Pauline theology was forgotten and replaced" (*Essays,* 93). The blame for this deterioration is laid by Käsemann upon the growing influence, emanating from Jerusalem, of the Jewish Christian leaders who tamed down the Pauline view of charisma and woodenly replaced it with the traditional Jewish notion of ordination, which had "the same meaning as it has in Judaism: it is the bestowal of the Spirit and it empowers those who receive it to administer the *depositum fidei* . . ." (*Essays,* 87). Käsemann concludes that Paul is later portrayed in Acts *as if* he were setting up presbyteries and trying to legitimate church order and apostolic succession as the guarantor of tradition, and Peter is later shown *as if* he were bestowing the apostolic blessing, inspecting churches, commissioning pastors, and participating in the laying on of hands. All of this Käsemann thinks was based upon a "fabricated chain of tradition" which "cannot possibly be harmonized" with Paul's theology, and even stands "in the starkest contradiction to it" (*Essays,* 87–92). He concludes his influential essay on "Paul and Nascent Catholicism" with this dismal irony: "The connection between Paul and the later period rested largely on misunderstanding" (*Essays,* 26).

This direction set by Bultmann and Käsemann (which can be detected earlier in the work of Rudolf Sohm and Martin Dibelius), is subsequently echoed by numerous contemporary New Testament scholars, from among whom I choose as a representative voice one who is often considered a moderate, mediating figure, Günther Bornkamm. Although Bornkamm makes the disclaimer that we would "do well not to censure the later writings in the New Testament canon by the theological standards of the previous age, or even of a later one," he nonetheless proceeds to do just that. Second Peter, he says, is "distinctly inferior to Paul's eschatology." "It is no longer the expression of a living faith. Not even the few impressive phrases it contains are enough to deceive the reader."[4] The letter of James he considers hardly an improvement, for in it "faith is relegated so far into the background that we are tempted to ask if this letter was originally a Christian writing at all" (*NTGW,* 120). In the Pastoral Epistles he sees reflected only "a bourgeois ideal of Christian morality" (*NTGW,* 115).

This depressing majority position was much earlier expressed by Rudolf Sohm's radical view that *any* ecclesiastical rule or law is contradictory to the very nature of the believing community. Bultmann fatefully agreed with Sohm's conception of the Church "as a society constituted not by a code of law but by the sway of the Spirit. [Sohm] is right, further in maintaining that the congregation, so understanding itself, needs no law; in fact *that legal regulation contradicts the Church's nature*" (*TNT II,* 97ff.). One might dismiss such a view as the petty, partisan polemics of Protestant individualism were it not for the fact that this view has been widely adopted by influential New Testament scholars, with the post-Bultmannians still exercising a broad hegemony among New Testament scholars in Europe and America.

When I began to ask how I had adopted the attitude that these later letters are of minimal theological importance, it dawned on me how deeply I, along with many others, have been affected by a strong tradition of highly esteemed New

[4] Günther Bornkamm, *The New Testament: A Guide to Its Writings,* trans. R.H. and Ilse Fuller (Philadelphia: Fortress Press, 1973), p. 127. Subsequent references to this work will be indicated in the text by *NTGW.*

Testament scholarship, very existentialist in its psychological predispositions, that has, in the name of objective historical scholarship, carried on a constant polemic against the tradition-nurturing and proto-catholic impulses of the New Testament—against its struggle with heresy, its attempt to develop an ordained succession of ministry, and its primitive attempts at church order.

This is no place to stretch a dreary string of supportive quotations in order further to establish the point, easily conceded by most knowledgeable New Testament scholars, that the prevailing opinion is that the Pastoral and General Epistles represent a depressing deterioration of earlier, vibrant New Testament theology, and are far less important to us than Paul or the Fourth Gospel or the Synoptics. Our task is rather to try to assess this consensus and its long-range consequences for our contemporary ailments in theology and ministry.

Under the tutelage of this critical school, chronological priority has come to mean theological priority, and its inverse to imply inevitable deterioration. The canon within the canon has thus been subtly redefined by historical critical scholars, first by establishing a late chronology for these writings, then by declaring unfavorably on their pseudonymity, and finally by casting them into a kind of decanonized limbo by pronouncing their theology patently inferior.

Those familiar with the history of Protestantism, but less so with the recent history of the critical study of scripture, might imagine that Protestant scholars would be vigorously defending canonical scripture (following the Reformation principle of *sola scriptura*), and taking for granted the authority of the canon universally affirmed by classical Protestant and Catholic traditions. A closer inspection reveals that these scholars are prone to think quite idiosyncratically about "the canon within the canon," and when the dust has settled the operating assumption is usually that these doctrinal questions are to be decided essentially on the grounds either of chronological priority, or by means of comparison with normative Paulinism, and thus canonicity itself has subtly become purely a matter of current (often faddish) historical-critical judgment! Käsemann, whose language tends to be more volatile than the others, resorts to the image of "freeing God" from the "imprisonment" of the canon (*Essays,* 105). For Käsemann, the function of the New Testament canon is less to constitute the foundation of the unity of the church than merely to "provide the basis for the multiplicity" of its confessions, which he believes to be enmeshed in "irreconcilable theological contradictions" (*Essays,* 100). Such statements, which would have been rejected out of hand by classical Protestant theologians, have of late taken on the solemn air of moral authority in some quarters of the community of biblical scholars, which not surprisingly is in danger of becoming ever more estranged from the living mainstream of the worshipping Christian communities they wish to serve.

Our steady hope in all this has been that the historians would make unprejudiced judgments about chronological priority and documentary authenticity, unaffected by hidden preconceptions. We have watched them assign their priorities, first to Paul, then to the Synoptics and John, and last (and clearly least) to these later writings, often pejoratively called "subapostolic" or "pseudo-Pauline" or "later pseudonymous writings." The hidden switch in this is that this order of priority directly corresponds with a silent predisposition of the tendency out of which all of these writers come, namely, the familiar polemic of the early Luther against medieval Catholicism, which becomes deceptively reread back into the New Testament. These esteemed historical experts thus solemnly rehearse the jaded Protestant myth that the earliest Christian communities had the purest doctrine, and that soon afterward the church "fell" into "organizational rigidities" and "catholic distortions." So part of the task of contemporary biblical scholarship is to battle the historical self-deceptions of New Testament exegetes who, under the guise of emptying themselves of prejudices, have reintroduced into biblical interpretation one of the most familiar of all Protestant prejudices, and under the presumption of historical objectivity have simply restated the tiresome sixteenth-century rhetoric against the catholicizing tendency. In correcting this trajectory, we must not oppose historical critical scholarship, but rather look for a less self-deceptive form of it. Historical criticsm must continue to do its work, but what it can never do is act as an authority for canonization. Historians do not have the authority to judge what is and is not canonical scripture. Only the church, in ecumenical consensus, can make that judgment, as it did in its earliest period of formation.

Largely unnoticed in this polemic is the fact that this most recent pattern of canonical revisionism is hardly a new challenge for the Christian tradition. These efforts are strikingly similar to those of Marcion, the second-century heretic who proposed an abridged canon dominated by Paul, or portions of Paul, sharply rejecting the Pastoral and General letters, admitting only a recension of the Gospel of Luke, and rejecting the other three Evangelists. In his determined attempt to rid the church of what he regarded as un-Pauline ideas and remnants of Jewish influence, however, Marcion indirectly influenced the early church to respond by distinguishing between authentic and spurious documents, and in this sense became a major (though indirect) factor in the development of the traditional canon, which, of course, steadfastly embraced the Pastoral and General Epistles.

When we allow ourselves to be addressed by these letters, however, we discover to our amazement that they represent not a deterioration but a marvelously spirited, vital, and maturing phase of early Christian theological development. They struggle with the meaning of ordination, the continuity and stability of the tradition, the nature of the pastoral office, the criteria for doctrinal definition, and the distinction between heterodoxy and orthodoxy—all issues that face us today. These are problems that could not have been taken up until the church had gained several decades of experience, and had faced up to the reality that it would have to continue to deal with developing history, governmental authority, and serious challenges to it from within and from without.

The Reversal of Decanonization

Having sketched the problem, what can we do to overcome it? What benefits are we likely to experience by rescuing the Pastoral and General Epistles from this strange status of unofficial decanonization? How is the context in which these letters were written similar to the context of our post-modern dilemmas of theology and ministry?

These vital questions cannot be answered in a few neat sentences, and indeed they must remain on the agenda of theology until they are clearly worked through, but I will attempt at least an initial, minimal answer, which I hope will be improved upon with continued debate.

We will benefit by the study of the Pastoral and General

Epistles today because they represent a maturing, not a degenerating, phase of early Christian theological development. The crucial question before the churches then was: How, in a period of cross-cultural pluralism, syncretism, political alienation, and vast historical mutation, is it possible to pass the tradition learned from the earliest Christians on to succeeding generations, how teach it accurately without distortions, and how defend it against interpretations that would profoundly diminish it? Whether the tradition even *could* be trans-generationally communicated in a period of widespread social disruption was a life and death question, and it remains problematic today. It reveals a tedious lack of imagination to conclude that their interest in historical continuity, unity, and tradition (which they solved successfully by means of ordination, the clear definition of apostolic teaching, a fierce struggle against heresy, and a stable church order) represented a disastrous setback in theology. If they had not done their job well in the period of the Pastoral and General Epistles, we would not be reading the rest of the New Testament now.

I do not imply that Paul or the Evangelists deserve any less study, but only that these pastoral writings deserve relatively more, partly to correct their long neglect, and partly because they speak so poignantly to our current pastoral struggles with anomie, social upheaval, antinomianism, and gnosticism.

How do contemporary theology and ministry stand to benefit from the recovery of these later writings of the New Testament? The answer is best expressed by framing a series of seven dilemmas of contemporary Christianity, and by then letting selected texts of the Pastoral and General Epistles answer for themselves.

Keep in mind, as you read these texts, that they are, in the view of ancient ecumencial Christianity, not merely objects of historical interest, but Word of God. It is not we who examine them, but the texts that examine us. Try to follow Kierkegaard's suggestion: Read these words as if they were a long-awaited letter from someone you love very much, who through this letter was asking you to do something concrete and specific.

1. Do the cultural upheavals we are now going through tend to make absurd the life of faith? Might the Christian inheritance be despoiled? How do our present difficulties put us in touch with the struggle of the Old Testament prophets?

> From Peter, apostle of Jesus Christ, to those of God's scattered people who lodge for a while in Pontus, Galatia, Cappadocia, Asia, and Bithynia. . . . Praise be to the God and Father of our Lord Jesus Christ, who in his great mercy gave us new birth into a living hope by the resurrection of Jesus Christ from the dead! The inheritance to which we are born is one that nothing can destroy or spoil or wither. . . . This is cause for great joy, even though now you smart for a little while, if need be, under trials of many kinds. Even gold passes through the assayer's fire, and more precious than perishable gold is faith which has stood the test. . . . This salvation was the theme which the prophets pondered and explored, those who prophesied about the grace of God awaiting you. They tried to find out what was the time, and what the circumstances, to which the spirit of Christ in them pointed, foretelling the sufferings in store for Christ and the splendours to follow; and it was disclosed to them that the matter they treated of was not for their time but for yours. And now it has been openly announced to you through preachers who brought you the Gospel in the power of the Holy Spirit sent from heaven. These are things that angels long to see into (1 Peter 1:1–12).

2. How are we to deal with the information overload and doctrinal pluralism in the religious sphere, so as to be able to grasp afresh the simplicity of faith in the God who loves sinners?

From Paul . . . to Timothy . . .: When I was starting for Macedonia, I urged you to stay on at Ephesus. You were to command certain persons to give up teaching erroneous doctrines and studying those interminable myths and genealogies, which issue in mere speculation and cannot make known God's plan for us, which works through faith. The aim and object of this command is the love which springs from a clean heart, from a good conscience, and from faith that is genuine. Through falling short of these, some people have gone astray into a wilderness of words. They set out to be teachers of the moral law, without understanding either the words they use or the subjects about which they are so dogmatic. . . . Here are words you may trust, words that merit full acceptance: "Christ Jesus came into the world to save sinners"; and among them I stand first. But I was mercifully dealt with for this very purpose, that Jesus Christ might find in me the first occasion for displaying all his patience, and that I might be typical of all who were in future to have faith in him and gain eternal life (1 Tim. 1:1–16).

3. Should Christian teaching be based upon personal, experiential authority, scripture, tradition, or a balanced synthesis of all these factors?

You, my son, have followed, step by step, my teaching and my manner of life, my resolution, my faith, patience, and spirit of love, and my fortitude under persecutions and sufferings—all that I went through at Antioch, at Iconium, at Lystra, all the persecutions I endured; and the Lord rescued me out of them all. Yes, persecution will come to all who want to live a godly life as Christians, whereas wicked men and charlatans will make progress from bad to worse, deceiving and deceived. But for your part, stand by the truths you have learned and are assured of. Remember from whom you learned them; remember that from early childhood you have been familiar with the sacred writings which have power to make you wise and lead you to salvation through faith in Christ Jesus. Every inspired scripture has its use for teaching the truth and refuting error, or for reformation of manners and discipline in right living, so that the man who belongs to God may be efficient and equipped for good work of every kind (2 Tim. 3:10–17).

4. Amid our present condition of alienation, can we learn to pray and persevere by trusting in God in a way that still seeks to be responsible for the neighbor in works of love and social engagement?

From James, a servant of God and the Lord Jesus Christ. Greetings to the Twelve Tribes dispersed throughout the world (James 1:1). A word with you, you who say, "Today or tomorrow we will go off to such and such a town and spend a year there trading and making money." Yet you have no idea what tomorrow will bring. Your life, what is it? You are no more than a mist, seen for a little while and then dispersing. What you ought to say is: "If it be the Lord's will, we shall live to do this or that" (4:13–15). Do not deceive yourselves, my friends. All good giving, every perfect gift, comes from above, from the Father of the lights of heaven. With him there is no variation, no play of passing shadows (1:16–17). My brothers, whenever you have to face trials of many kinds, count yourselves supremely happy, in the knowledge that such testing of your faith breeds fortitude, and if you give fortitude full play you will go on to complete a balanced character that will fall short in nothing. If any of you falls short in wisdom, he should ask God for it and it will be given him, for God is a generous giver who neither refuses nor reproaches anyone. But he must ask in faith, without a doubt in his mind; for the doubter is like a heaving sea ruffled by the wind. A man of that kind must not expect the Lord to give him anything; he is double-minded, and never can keep a steady course

8

The Cusp of the Second Millennium

I SUGGEST a simple test for showing that the innocent words *new* and *change* actually function like potent magic words in our current vocabulary, and with particularly surprising force in religious conversations. Go to your next theological discussion or study group and accurately count the number of times *new* and *change* are used. Then ask yourself, was there any instance in which these words were used in a pejorative sense? And how often did it occur that the persons using them silently assumed that their hearers would also assume that new = good, change = improvement; that if something new could be identified it would *by definition* bring about a better situation; or if some undeveloped process developed it would *thereby* (!) constitute a "step ahead"; or if something merely changed it would imply a moral advancement or a virtue of some kind?

If your count is like mine, I think you will discover that these words function in our time almost exactly like magic words have functioned in earlier societies. Some conversants will use the magic words incessantly, sprinkling them generously in most every religious reference. Others use the magic words somewhat as a kid uses body torque while playing pinball as if to try to persuade the ball to go a certain way until the "tilt" sign lights up. Academics may prefer more distinguished synonyms, such as *emergent, innovative, revolutionary,* or *metamorphosis,* but the magic is still there. Eyes light up, bells ring, money changes hands—in fact, the overall effect of the magic words in some circles is very like a pinball fantasy victory.

The surest move toward postmodern theological consciousness consists in following this simple maxim: Quit using *new* and *change* as magic words. Quitting cold turkey is, of course, most difficult, but when it can be done the reversal of consciousness is felt dramatically. I know of no better therapy for unconscious faddism.

By the same logic, modernity also has its *bad* magic words: Anything that looks "old hat" or "antiquated" or "rigid" or "traditional" will be subtly linked implicitly with evils to be avoided, vicious repressions that hold us down, powers of darkness.

Check it out for yourself. Plot it in two columns on a sheet of paper, listing the news and olds, the changes and intransigencies, the plusses and minuses. It comes closer to twentieth-century sympathetic magic than anything I know of. Like all magic, it is thought to work most efficaciously where its effectiveness is not questioned or suspected. So, if you are brave enough occasionally to raise stubborn questions about the realistic potency of these magic words, be prepared for some groans, for you may touch a tender spot. One need only ask:

"Does *new* mean *good,* in your view?" and the conversation can never be the same.

The Revisionists

Fantasize, if you will, a large group of energetic scholars who call themselves "Islamic theologians," but who never pray, seldom bother to read the Quran, who in their private moments derisively mock Mohammed and do clever pantomimes of him that suggest that he was little more than a silly, neurotic egotist, *yet* who nonetheless insist vehemently that they represent the authentic tradition of Islamic spirituality.

Suppose that the secret passion of these scholars is actually the study of Freud. They have taken carefully selected passages of the Quran and medieval Islamic texts and radically reinterpreted them in a Freudian fashion, showing their oedipal ambivalences, repressed sexuality, totemic symbolism, the cathexis of wish formations, subtle forms of sublimation, and so on, so that the final result was a blatant Freudianization of Islam. Of course, all the moral imperatives would then have to go, the sociological substance of the Islamic tradition would obviously be found dispensible, all ideas of revelation would have to be dismissed. Yet suppose these scholars held fast to the pretense that they were the true arbiters of Islamic teaching. Don't laugh too quickly; for such a reversal is entirely possible (and in fact I would not be surprised if a group of scholars in some Iranian university were not currently working along just such "constructive" lines).

My question is, If you were advising a young theological student who had become fascinated with Islam, and who wanted to go abroad to learn all he could about the spirit of genuine Islam, would you even consider sending him to these "Islamic Theologians"? No. You would advise him to go instead to one of the renowned historical centers of traditional Islamic prayer, legal study, archival deposits, and religious reflection. Most of all you would hope that he would somehow find his way into a vibrant, pulsating community of genuine Islamic faith, so as to get in touch with the tremendous creative energies of Islam through the centuries. And if he had heard somewhere of the Freudian Muslims and was curiously fascinated by them, you would wisely advise him that, if he were interested merely in pseudo-Islamic curiosities, they might be given some attention, but if he were interested the central tradition of Islam devoutly believed by millions, he would do well to understand it historically as a living community of prayer, instead of a twisted plaything seen through the heavily coated lens of modernity.

Yet something like Freudianized Islam has proliferated in modern Christianity. We have seen the language of Christianity tamed by the civil religionists, neatly pruned by the logical positivists, "dehistoricized" by the existentialists, "deabsolutized" by the process theologians, naturalized by the behaviorists, sentimentalized by the situation ethicists, freaked-out by the drug-oriented spiritualists, secularized by the "death of God" partisans, politicized by the social activists, and set free from all bonds by the sexual liberationists. In each case, they cheerlessly rebaptized Christianity in the triune name of the nineteenth, twentieth, and twenty-first centuries. (Visualize each movement being solemnly immersed three times under water with the numbers of the three centuries in each plunge being gravely intoned by psychiatrists, gurus, or spiritual adepts).

But Christianity is not now and has not since the seventeenth century been fairly judged exclusively by its *au courant* manifestations; rather, it is to be properly judged and understood by its primitive formation, and by those periods of its historical development that have given the most scrupulous attention to the original vitalities of its primitive formation. It is not to be judged even by what a majority of contemporary theologians might say is true Christianity if they forgetfully depart from scripture and ancient ecumenical tradition.

A Reversal of Consciousness

An unexpected learning occurred the day I had to pack up my books for shipment to the distant spot where I was to spend a change-of-pace research year. I was to be away from my own personal library for an entire year, a prospect that gives any bibliophile teeth-rattling separation anxieties. I was force to make harsh choices about which volumes I would take and which to leave behind. If I shipped too many books, the cost would be atrocious. As I began to make my second and third round eliminations, an astonishing pattern became apparent to me: I was picking Aeschylus, Clement of Alexandria, Epictetus, Tertullian, Nemesius, John Chrysostom, Augustine, Boethius, Dante, Hugh of St. Victor, Anselm, and so on. Many of these books I had already read before, but they seemed more important to take with me. Finally the shock hit me: There were *no* books among my final selections from the twentieth century! The most recent ones in my shipment list were Horace Bushnell, Friedrich Nietzsche, and Eliabeth Cady Stanton. Did that mean that I was bored with twentieth-century literature? Hardly, for I teach several courses, and enjoy teaching them, in twentieth-century thought. The truth is, however, that I found the premodern writers more personally significant for my growth, more crucial for my personal being, than the full range of scientific and literary achievements of the twentieth century.

I learned something pivotally important about myself on that fateful day. It felt as though the second Christian millennium was already over for me spiritually. It was as if it had burned itself out twenty years or so before its expected demise. If I had to assign a date that I became a "postmodern" (similar to the way the frontier revivalists used to speak of the exact day they were converted), I think it would be that bright, sunny day when I chose the books I most needed, and most certainly wanted with me, and discovered to my astonishment that if push came to shove I *could* do without the twentieth-century material altogether, but that I could *not* seem to do without Hippolytus, Aquinas, Nicolas of Cusa, *Theologia Germanica,* Maimonides, Pascal, and Kierkegaard.

The word *cuspis* (Latin) means a pointed end or projection formed by converging curves. In horoscopy, the term *cusp* refers to the tail end of one period or the beginning of another, often a time of uncertainty and volatility. One might say that we are rapidly coming to the cusp of the second Christian millennium. It offers us the exceptional possibility of rethinking the meaning of the first two millennia and the challenge to prepare ourselves for the third.

These words of John Watson from the Beecher Lectures of 1896 at Yale seem aimed directly at us today:

> For a quarter of a century at least, the intellectual resources of the church have been withdrawn from the study of dogma (with, of course, some brilliant exceptions) and devoted to criticism. . . . The ministers of today have been trained in this age and baptized into

> its spirit. We have shared the hopes and endeavours, we have felt the doubts and anxieties of our time, and we can now frankly tell our people its faults and fruits.
>
> Criticism has offended the church by its *pretentiousness,* for its preachers were apt to speak as if they had a new gospel. Of course they had nothing, and could have nothing, of the kind. They have given a large amount of information and they have removed some traditions, but a message for the soul criticism can never offer. . . . Criticism has also sinned through *uncharitableness;* for some of the pioneers of the new school have forgotten good manners and have not carried themselves respectfully to the past. While a discoverer in physics is ever grateful for the work done by his predecessors, and corrects their mistakes with humility, recognizing that he stands on their shoulders and that his results will also one day be revised, the biblical critic has been inclined to treat the old scholarship with unconcealed contempt, and to expose its errors with malignant satisfaction.[1]

The theological situation in the last quarter of the twentieth century does not differ substantially from the last quarter of the nineteenth, except that the incipient habits Watson described in 1896 have now become institutionalized, normative, and professionalized.

We have witnessed in these waning stages of the twentieth century a powerful polemic against what has been called *repression* of many kinds—sexual repression (Freud), class repression (Marx), and political repression (Marcuse). We now have seen enough of these polemicists to realize at least two things: (1) that what is called *repression* is often either the legitimate protest of conscience or a carefully balanced and hard-won equilibrium of social traditioning, and (2) the social and psy-

[1] John Watson, "The New Dogma," *The Cure of Souls* (New York: Dodd, Mead and Co., 1896), pp. 140-42.

chological alternatives that are proposed in the name of counterrepression are themselves often even more profoundly oppressive both to conscience and human community. This is one of the most harsh but most certain learnings of the pilgrimage of postmodern youth. Because they could not learn it from history, they were forced to learn from hard experience that the high-sounding, low-slugging polemic against repression is itself often unexpectedly even more repressive.

Twentieth-century theology has too cheaply and prematurely sided with this oversimplified Freudian and Marxian polemic against social and psychological repression. But this is merely the tip of the iceberg. The whole eros of twentieth-century theology, following well-established trends of nineteenth-century religious accommodationism, has been directed toward finding some convenient means of legitimization in the presence of modernity. By now, many of us are experiencing a gnawing disenchantment with the disenchantments of modernity. But if the time has come to spoil the spoilers and to debunk the debunkers, let it proceed without malice and above all in good humor. This work has been begun by David Tracy, Will Herberg, Peter Berger, Michael Novak, Andrew Greeley, and others, but so far it has only scratched the surface, and the critique has not achieved the levels of comedy or irony that the situation richly invites.

Wishing not to be misunderstood, I happily confess that I am a modern man still fascinated with the twentieth century and feel fortunate to be a part of it technologically, although I keep wondering to what depth my soul has been traded away. The scientific and technological achievements of modern life are so impressive, even awesome, that they remind us that all our mechanisms can be just as easily turned against justice and humanization as toward them. Christianity need not think backward technologically, but all of this spectacular progress in technology does not imply an inevitable ethical or spiritual progress. We are deluded when we extrapolate the "success" of the internal combustion engine and atomic power (as if they were unmixed blessings) so as to imagine that they represent a fated momentum toward unending spiritual progress.

Admittedly we would all prefer to go to a dentist with up-to-date equipment than one with antiquated medieval pliers, and we would rather travel cross country by air than horse. But that does not imply that new ideas are by their newness better; or that our grandchildren, because they come later in time, are *ipso facto* destined to be morally more aware than we are; or that we are spiritually more advanced than our grandparents. It is that not-so-subtle skip in logic, the progressivist *non sequitur,* that has led modernity astray and in the process deceived contemporary ministry into indescribable fantasies.

The paradigm of "social planning" (and of theology modeled after images of social planning) has exercised undue influence on religious reflection. This paradigm assumes that a single creative person can create on the drawing board a better idea of society or a better design for a social process than can history itself (that is, the actual meshing wills of specific people struggling under the concrete limitations of unfolding history). Elitist social architects assume that the tough part is getting the right idea, and the easy part is the implementation of it in actual social arrangements. So social planning (and theologies based upon it) quickly becomes an idea factory, more or less dismissing the actualities of history and the real people that inhabit it. The university establishment has fed on this fantasy, assuming that individuals looking at history from highly abstract and distanced angles would be able easily to achieve more precise and better forms of social reasoning than the actual historical process itself. How pretentious, to assume that the lone individual is wiser and better than the complex determinants of a living traditionary process. Yet nothing is more characteristic of theology at the end of the second millennium than this elitist fantasy. Virtually a direct opposite of the paradigm of social planning is the implicit theological method of orthodoxy.

Orthodoxy as Theological Method

By "theological method," theologians usually mean the ground rules by which theology is supposed to proceed. Debates on theological method often come down to the question of authority: What kinds of statements are to be admitted in discourse about God, and on what authority?

Christian orthodoxy of the first Christian millennium proceeded with this implicit theological method: Theology speaks of the triune God on the basis of the eventful self-disclosure of God in history, made known in scripture, rigorously reflected upon by reason, and experienced personally through a living liturgical tradition, whose faith seeks an understanding of itself in each new cultural context. Christian social experience has shown that our own private, individual experiences and reasonings need the constant guidance of scripture and tradition in order to be animated wholesomely by the revelation of God in universal history, in the people of Israel and in Jesus Christ. Far from denying or neglecting reason and experience, orthodoxy wishes to embody them in and through a living tradition. Accordingly, reason and experience rise to their higher possibilities only in response to grace.

I am proposing in this agenda a return to the normative

self-restrictions that have prevailed in Christianity's first millennium. But why the first millennium? Not because this period was intrinsically more exciting than other eras, or its advocates more brilliant, but because of its close adherence to apostolic faith and because a more complete ecumenical consensus was achieved in that period than any period since, a consensus that in fact has been subsequently affirmed by Protestant, Catholic, and Greek Orthodox traditions. If the second Christian millennium ends in a denial of the first Christian millennium, it amounts to a denial of its own history and to a radical splitting in two of its identity. The task of postmodern orthodoxy is to restore integrity to the historical self-understanding of Christianity, to rediscover what makes Christians of the late twentieth century spiritually more like Christians of the fifth or fifteenth century than even like admired persons of their own hometown or family who have not heard God's good news. Part of the joy of historical discovery in Christian theology is the growing awareness of this affinity with persons who lived in very different cultural periods than we live in, but whose faith was shaped by lively participation in Christ whose love remains the same yesterday, today, and forever.

The thrust of orthodox theological method is seen in its own statements about *why* the councils were convened: not to "remove the ancient landmarks" but to "remain steadfast in the testimonies and authority of the holy and approved fathers" (Third Council of Constantinople); to "drive away the laughter of the heterodox" (Chalcedon); "to unite the churches again and to bring the Synod of Chaldedon together with the three earlier, to universal acceptance." "We hold that faith which our Lord Jesus Christ, the true God, delivered to his holy apostles, and through them to the holy churches, and which they who after them were holy fathers and doctors, handed down to the people credited to them" (Second Council of Constantinople). The precise focus was on accurate transmission, not innovation. The council fathers were especially sensitive to points at which the faith was under attack: "Let us be in all things of one mind, of one heart, when the faith, which is one, is attacked. Let the whole body grieve and mourn in common with us" (Ephesus). Later Luther, despite his reputation as a reformer, instructed his pastors to "avoid changes or variations in the text" of liturgy or catechism: "Adopt one form, adhere to it, and use it repeatedly year after year. [For people] are easily confused if a teacher employs one form now and another form—perhaps with the intention of making improvements—later on."

The theological method of orthodoxy proceeds not by asking how we *feel* or about which theologian's view is most brilliant or about futuristic probability estimates or about whether the faith can adjust itself to various world views, but rather by asking a simple question: What in fact did the apostles teach? What is the baptism into which we have been baptized? What is the tradition we have received? Taken seriously, this question simplifies the theological effort considerably, sharpens the focus, and hedges against diversions. After hearing the Tome of Leo, the fathers at Chalcedon cried out, "This is the faith of the fathers, this is the faith of the Apostles. So we all believe, thus the orthodox believe." They intuited it, knew it, remembered it, and tested it by its correspondence with the apostolic teaching.

"It is not necessary that traditions and ceremonies be in all places one, or utterly like," the Anglican Thirty-Nine Articles wisely affirmed, "for at all times they have been divers, and may be changed according to the diversity of countries, times, and [human] manners." The same article gently chides the intemperate spirit who irascibly breaks church traditions even when they are not in conflict with scriptures, since such iconoclasm injures respect for authority generally, and "wounds the conscience of the weak brethren." In the relatively tolerant central tradition of Anglican orthodoxy, we see a wise balance of grace and freedom, apostolicity and cultural imagination, doctrinal firmness yet tolerant respect for the variety of social traditions. The English church tradition happily embraced this tolerant pluralism, and then shipped it to America, where it has borne delicious fruits. Yet in its liberalizing and pietistic American forms, it has tended to lose the rich liturgical and doctrinal center that had been the beacon light to previous experimental generations.

Can the theological method of ancient ecumenical orthodoxy be directly and straightforwardly adopted by postmodern orthodoxy? Probably not directly, but its intention stands as a significant corrective to the distortions we have been experiencing. For it wishes more than anything to have a good, clear memory. It understands itself to be charged with the care of the apostolic tradition and with responding to challenges to the tradition with an ecumenical consensus guided by the Holy Spirit. It was not in search of a consensus of current opinion, however, but rather for the apostolic consensus that itself had been repeatedly reaffirmed and defined by the previous ecumenical councils.

When we penetrate our pastoral façades, we often find that the liberal Protestant minister has a hidden orthodox side and a revealed modern side. We enjoy displaying the public liberal face and posture, but deep inside us somehow is the appropriation into our personality structures of those ancient ideas and symbols of the apostolic tradition and trinitarian Christian orthodoxy. The Christological images in the hymns of the church are mixed in the marrow of our bones. We liberals have received the *consensus fidelium* probably more through hymns and, to some degree, through prayer and liturgy than we have through preaching. These ancient images resonate in our consciousness and memory, however up to date we wish to appear. They tell us who we are, revealing to us the depths of our lostness, our moral situation before God that we neglect to the detriment of our souls.

We know all this. How strange it is, then, that we so easily put down that side of ourselves, deny it, disavow it, do not let it *be.* Scratch the surface of the average liberal Protestant pastor and you will find underneath the public, nonprudish, permissive, "liberated" side that frowns about hunger and smiles about sex, there is a deeper hunger for the core message of God's radical, saving, judging love for humankind in Jesus Christ, the risen and living Lord, and an awareness of the holy God present in our midst to judge our idolatries and forgive our sins.

We see also the limitations of orthodoxy: its temptation, despite its best intuitions, to view all reality from a limited vantage point; its intolerances and inequalities; its pretense and pride. But at its heart, we know that classical Christianity is wiser and better than its modern alternatives. As enlightenment liberals we have expended enormous energies trying to escape from the overweening demands of orthodoxy. Since liberalism is a tradition against tradition, we have been through a long negative-reinforcement training process to teach us a kind of general distrust of doctrinal orthodoxy. Somewhere deep inside, however, we know that we do not have anything better to offer, and that our experimentations depend upon the larger frame of reference in which to experiment which orthodoxy has nurtured and protected.

The Interpersonal Wilderness

With joy and sadness, we have watched the last century of the second millennium unfold decade by decade. Having made excessive promises for human self-deliverance, the twentieth century now faces the demoralization of its own unfulfilled promises. There are many angles of vision from which to behold the failure of modern psychologies, philosophies, sciences, and politics, but the most revealing nexus of these failures, I think, lies in the impotence of modernity to sustain interpersonal covenants, to nurture responsible commitment in enduring associations and intimacies. In part, I am talking about modernity's failure to understand marriage as the most transparent clue to the failure of modern consciousness, but we could also talk about the failure of friendships and the failure of politics. Wherever we look in the interpersonal sphere we see the failure of naturalistic, quasi-humanistic values to nurture and sustain just interpersonal relationships and responsible covenant love. It is most easily seen in the popular image of marriage as if marriage were solely a cost–benefit calculus instead of a solemn promise. With that reasoning, when costs increase, the relationship ends. Here the sexual liberationists, and many psychotherapists, despite the best intentions, have been as much a part of the problem as of its solution. The disastrous social results of modern autonomous individualism are strewn everywhere about us in the social scene. The increase in crime, social pathology, personal violence, rape, and anomie has its roots in the loss of the primary center of social formation, the family, and the diaspora of the family has its roots in the abandonment of solemnly covenanted and durably bonded matrimony. At heart, it is a theological failure, not merely a social, political, or psychological miscalculation or "setback."

I am not an alarmist about the long-term future of marriage, not only because three out of four divorces end in marriage, but more because the hunger for covenant fidelity is structured into human sexuality. And I do not wish to take a strictly rigorous moralistic line against divorce that admits of no exceptions, for some persons grow magnificently through these breaks. But I cannot let the subject of modernity go without attempting a pathos-laden observation that I find extremely difficult to articulate in the depth that I experience its importance without appearing overly simplistic or judgmental. It is about divorce: The recent history of divorce is *the* key sign of the failure of modernity to sustain covenant accountability in the interpersonal sphere. Modernity has come to the "profound insight" that marriage is "a piece of paper," a superego intrusion, an establishment voyeurism on "two people in love." When marriage is no longer a solemnly bonded promise before God with the intent of irrevocability, it turns quickly into merely a moment-to-moment hedonic calculus that is as flippantly rejected as it is entered into.

We have learned much in modernity, but we have not learned what the Old Testament calls *chesed,* the enduring, steadfast, covenant love of God that does not quit loving just because the cost–benefit ratio is lowered. Sexually what that means for the Western moral tradition has always been and still is monogamous, enduring, covenant bonding in sexuality. We have not learned that from our society, bent as it is toward individualistic self-assertion. We are now bedeviled by the growing awareness that we cannot sustain our family covenants on the basis of purely hedonistic values or amoral autonomy. The interpersonal consequences of modern self-assertive narcissism are not just a minor disorder or regrettable error, but on the whole they are more accurately described as calamitous. The reason this has not been sooner recognized by avant-garde religious leaders is precisely because their accommodationist predilections have severely reduced critical perception. For modernity still persists in fantasizing history as a progressive evolution toward ever-better forms wherein our most vexing moral ills will finally be cured through improved education, technology, and moral suasion. If you begin with these ideological blinders, you will certainly fail to see the social disasters that will follow in your wake, because you have already decided that such disasters cannot really persist in a truly modern world with all its "obvious" intellectual, moral, and educational resources.

The Winter Temperament

The premise of this book is that it is possible for the core of classical Christian belief to stand in critical dialogue with modern personal and social hopes, but this cannot be a mere monologue, as it has recently been, in which classical Christianity listens without making its own positive contribution. It is in an effort to overcome the onesidedness of this conversation that I place special emphasis now upon the recovery of the Christian center. That does not imply an abandonment of the task of dialogue, but rather hopes in a deeper way for real dialogue.

I have spent most of my career working span by span on a bridge between psychology and religion. Just how incessantly preoccupied I have been with this theological bridge is clear, if from nothing else, from the titles of my previous books:

Kerygma and Counseling, Contemporary Theology and Psychotherapy, The Structure of Awareness, The Intensive Group Experience, After Therapy What?, Game Free, and *TAG: The Transactional Awareness Game.* After two decades of bridge building, however, it is finally dawning on me that the traffic is moving on the bridge only one way: from psychological speculations to rapt religious attentiveness. The conversation has been completely one-sided. Theology's listening to psychology has been far more accurate, empathic, and attentive than has psychology's listening to theology. I do not cease to hope for a viable two-way dialogue, but there is as little evidence that theology is ready to speak out in such a dialogue as there is that psychology is ready to listen. The bridge will not be built by the complete acquiescence of theology to the reductionist assumptions of psychology, or by relinquishing such key religious postulates as providence and resurrection.

We have been going, as Jeremiah (7:24) said, "backwards and not forwards." We eat, but are not satisfied (Lev. 26:26). We are technologically superior to premodernity, but not psychologically, morally, spiritually, and certainly not interpersonally. "He that soweth iniquity shall reap vanity" (Prov. 22:8, KJV). We moderns, having "sown the wind" are now "reaping the whirlwind" of interpersonal alienation and discontent. We have looked to the modern academic and clinical centers to tell the church what it is supposed to be doing, how it is best to understand itself, and what its values are, only to find that "if one blind man guides another they will both fall into the ditch" (Matt. 15:14). At the height of our supposed powers, we as moderns "stumble at noonday as in the night; we are in desolate places as dead men" (Isa. 59:10). Like Jeremiah, we behold the once-fruitful land that, contrary to all our expectations has become an interpersonal wilderness.

Sometimes it seems that only a few may survive the desolations of modernity. "God waited patiently in the days of Noah and the building of the ark, and in the ark a few persons . . . were brought to safety through the water" (1 Pet. 3:20). In that remnant will be only the hardiest and most realistic, even as the remnant that survived the destruction of Rome were the sons and daughters of the Christian martyrs of the second and third centuries.

It is the winter season for rigorous Christian teaching. But it has been through many winters before. It is time to cast off all things unessential, to drop leaves and branches that are no longer functional, to trim down for a long winter of survival, to reduce energies to the bare essentials in order to sustain the organism through the hazards of time. There is much stormy weather ahead. Only the hardiest may survive. Modernity is a winter season for classical Christianity. Spring will come, but only to those who have survived the winter.

We have heard a great deal recently about a theology of conviviality, the feast of fools, the laughter of God, the celebration of the body, a swinging confession for a swinging time—but we know better. Most modern religious talk about these themes has been under the sway of hedonistic philosophies that deal with suffering only by avoidance. Indeed, there is a joy in the Christian life that comes from discipline, a laughter that echoes even under winter's heaviest snows, a happiness that Christians know to be grounded in God's own joy over his creation. But it is never easily won or sustained without effort. Young Christians especially seem to sense that the season of modernity is a winter season and that it is time for conserving the essentials.

Epilogue: The Collage

THE INK remained bold and clear on an ancient papyrus manuscript. It had survived many centuries with thoughtful care, even though it had been repeatedly handled, breathlessly touched, and read aloud countless times by persons awed by its beauty and sacredness. But years ago the manuscript was set on a shelf, and then inadvertently pushed to the back, into a corner where it sat out decades of neglect. It was a drafty spot that subjected the delicate manuscript to harsh extremes of heat and cold. Dust accumulated. Mice nibbled at its edges. In time a steady unnoticed drip eventually made the ink wash and fade. Thinking it was nothing, a janitor tossed it out in the throwaway cart, which was then set outdoors for pickup just before a heavy rain, which caused the characters to wash away even more; one could hardly make them out.

Meanwhile a contemporary artist, rummaging through the bin looking for interesting materials for his newest collage, ran across this fascinating roll of fragile papyrus. He viewed it esthetically, as a lovely piece of antique parchment. He was especially attracted by its fine texture, its off-white color, the swirling flows of ghost-gray markings. Excitedly he carried the bundle home, spread it out, and decided instantly that it could serve as just the right backdrop material for a large collage that would significantly display twisted fragments of industrial junk and waste on the background of a lovely, ancient-looking surface.

Suppose that you and I became the proud owners of this collage, hung it in the most honored place, only later to discover, on closer inspection, that the sporadic markings of ink were actually complex hieroglyphs that proved to be an ancient sacred scripture, that held the promise of revealing significant insight into human history and destiny. What would then be our task? First, to try to remove painstakingly the heavy modern overlay without damaging the fragile script and then to restore the faded letters so as to make them visible and understandable again.

Many may still persist in viewing Christianity essentially as an object of aesthetic interest, a curious yet lovely modern collage, without reference to its historical identity, its power to redeem, or its radical claim on the human spirit. The happy task of theology is to rediscover and reveal the message underneath the garish modern overlay.

Appendix: Perennial Resources for Ministry

THIS appendix addresses the practical problem of building a personal, pastoral, or church library that will make available to the community of faith the key texts of classical Christian consciousness. Several obstacles stand in the way. Many key works are unavailable, some are available only in expensive editions, and even the ones that are available are often not left long on the shelves of bookstores, for understandable reasons. Stores that have some minimal stock in classical Christian writings often limit them to a particular denominational tradition or doctrinal perspective. So we must learn to order books.

Among classical Christian authors whose key works are either completely inaccessible, available only on rare book lists, or in completely inadequate translations are: Peter

Abelard, Albert the Great, Alexander of Hales, Bellarmine, Theodore Beza, Guillaume Farel, August Hermann Francke, Johann Gerhard, Jean Gerson, Hugh of St. Victor, John Knox, William Laud, Peter Lombard, Raymond Lull, Philipp Melanchthon, Luis de Molina, Papias, Theodore of Mopsuestia, and Nikolaus von Zinzendorf. The list could continue much further.

The happier side of this picture is that even though many classical texts are out of print, some are nonetheless available, many at an exceptionally low cost. The purpose of this bibliography is to help persons in ministry build a personal or church library of key classical texts without inordinate expense. The criteria I have applied in recommending the following are: list only primary sources in reliable editions; list only books in print, to save the reader's search time; keep costs down by preferring inexpensive or paperback editions to high cost reprints; limit the list to widely acknowledged classics, but attempt to express the full variety of central Christian traditions without partisan prejudices.

The result is encouraging. It is possible to build a "no frills" classical Christian library for fifty dollars (note entries preceded by †), and a church library can be reasonably well fitted, in terms of today's available options, for less than one hundred dollars (note entries preceded by ‡). The key, of course, is selective ordering, and an astute book retailer can be of immense help in placing these special orders. For the reader's convenience, books priced under five dollars when this list was compiled are marked with an asterisk (*). The list is organized chronologically, ending with anthologies and multivolume series.

Primary Sources of Classical Christianity

THE APOSTOLIC FATHERS

† *Early Christian Writings.* Translated by M. Staniforth. New York: Penguin Books, 1968.*

The Faith of the Early Fathers. Translated by W.A. Jurgens. Collegeville, Minn: Liturgical Press, 1970.

‡ *Apostolic Fathers, Justin Martyr and Ireneus.* Ante-Nicene Fathers, edited by A. C. Coxe, vol. 1. Grand Rapids, Mich.: Eerdmans Publishing Co., 1956.

Hermas, Tatian, Athenagoras, Theophilus, Clement of Alexandria. Ante-Nicene Fathers, vol. 2.

ANTE-NICENE FATHERS

† Chadwick, H., ed. *Alexandrian Christianity.* Library of Christian Classics, vol. 2. Philadelphia: Westminster Press, 1954.

Origen. *On First Principles.* Translated by G.W. Butterworth. Gloucester, Mass.: Peter Smith, 1966.

Tertullian, Parts I–III. Ante-Nicene Fathers, vol. 3.

Hippolytus, Cyprian, Caius, Novation, Appendix. Ante-Nicene Fathers, vol. 5.

‡ Greenslade, S.L., ed. *Early Latin Theology.* Library of Christian Classics, vol. 5, 1956.

MAJOR PATRISTIC WRITERS

‡ Athanasius, St. *Select Works and Letters.* Edited by A. Robertson. Nicene and Post-Nicene Fathers, 2nd series, vol. 4. Grand Rapids, Mich.: Eerdmans Publishing Co., 1956.

Sayings of the Desert Fathers. Translated by B. Ward. Kalamazoo, Mich.: Cistercian Publications, 1975.

Basil, St. *Letters and Select Works.* Edited by B. Jackson. Nicene and Post-Nicene Fathers, 2nd Series, vol. 8.

Cyril of Jerusalem, St. *Catechetical Lectures.* Edited by E.H. Gifford; and Gregory Nazianzen, St. *Orations and Letters.* Edited by C.G. Browne and J.E. Swallow. Nicene and Post-Nicene Fathers, 2nd Series, vol. 7.

Gregory of Nyssa. *Dogmatic Treatises.* Edited by V.W. Moore and H.A. Willson. Nicene and Post-Nicene Fathers, 2nd Series, vol. 5.

Eusebius. *The History of the Church.* Translated by G.A. Williamson. Minneapolis: Augsburg Publishing House, 1975.

Chrysostom, St. John. *In Praise of St. Paul.* Boston: Daughters of St. Paul, 1964.*

Chrysostom, St. John. *On the Priesthood; Ascetic Treatises; Select Homilies and Letters; Homilies on the Statues,* Nicene and Post-Nicene Fathers, 2nd Series, vol. 9.

† Augustine, St. *Confessions of St. Augustine.* Translated by E.B. Pusey. New York: Macmillan, 1961.*

† Augustine, St. *Enchiridion on Faith, Hope and Love.* Edited by H. Paolucci. Chicago: Henry Regnery Co., 1961.*

‡ Augustine, St. *St. Augustine: On Education.* Edited by G. Howie. Chicago: Henry Regnery Company, 1969.*

Augustine, St. *City of God.* Translated by J. Healey. New York: E.P. Dutton & Co., 1956.

‡ Augustine, St. *On Christian Doctrine.* Translated by D.W. Robertson. Indianapolis: Bobbs-Merrill Co., 1958.*

Augustine, St. *First Catechetical Instruction.* Translated by J.P. Christopher. New York: Paulist Press, 1946.*

Augustine, St. *Augustine: Early Writings.* Edited by J.H. Burleigh. Library of Christian Classics, vol. 6, 1953.

Augustine, St. *The Writings Against the Manichaeans and Against the Donatists.* Edited by A.H. Newman, R. Stothert, and C.D. Hartranft. Nicene and Post-Nicene Fathers, 2nd Series, vol. 4.

Jerome, St. *Letters and Select Works.* Edited by W.H. Fremantle. Nicene and Post-Nicene Fathers, 2nd Series, vol. 6.

Hilary of Poitiers, St. *Select Works.* Translated by E.W. Watson; and John of Damascus, St. *Exposition of the Orthodox Faith.* Translated by S.D.F. Salmond. Nicene and Post-Nicene Fathers, 2nd Series, vol. 9.

Ambrose, St. *Select Works and Letters.* Edited by H. de Romestin. Nicene and Post-Nicene Fathers, 2nd Series, vol. 10.

Severus, Sulpitius, *Works.* Edited by Alexander Roberts; Vincent of

Lerins. *Commonitory.* Edited by C.A. Heurtley; Cassian, John. *Works.* Edited by E.C.S. Gibson. Nicene and Post-Nicene Fathers, 2nd Series, vol. 11.

Feltoe, C.L., ed. *Leo the Great, Gregory the Great.* Part I, Works. Nicene and Post-Nicene Fathers, 2nd series, vol. 12.

‡ Boethius, *The Consolation of Philosophy.* Translated by V.E. Watts. New York: Penguin Books, 1976.*

Benedict St. *Rule.* Translated by J. McCann. Westminster, Md.: Christian Classics, Inc., 1972.*

Dionysius the Areopagite. *Divine Names and Mystical Theology.* Translated by C.E. Rolt. Naperville, Ill.: Alec R. Allenson, 1920.

† *The Seven Ecumenical Councils.* Edited by H.R. Percival. Nicene and Post-Nicene Fathers, 2nd Series, vol. 14.

CLASSICAL MEDIEVAL TEXTS

‡ Anselm, St. *Basic Writings.* Translated by S.N. Dean. La Salle, Ill.: Open Court Publishing Co., 1966.*

Fairweather, E., ed. *A Scholastic Miscellany: Anselm to Ockham.* Library of Christian Classics, vol. 10, 1956.

Bernard of Clairvaux. *Treatise on Loving God.* Kalamazoo, Mich.: Cistercian Publications, 1974.

‡ Francis of Assisi, St. *Writings.* Chicago: Franciscan Herald Press, 1964.*

‡ Bonaventura, St. *The Mind's Road to God.* Translated by G. Boas. Indianapolis: Bobbs-Merrill Co., 1953.*

Thomas Aquinas, St. *Nature and Grace, Selections from Summa Theologica.* Edited by A.M. Fairweather. Library of Christian Classics, vol. 11, 1954.

Thomas Aquinas, St. *Political Ideas of St. Thomas Aquinas.* Edited by D. Bigongiari. New York: Macmillan Publishing Co., 1973.*

Thomas Aquinas, St. *Providence and Predestination.* Translated by R.W. Mulligan. Chicago: Henry Regnery Co., 1975.

Thomas Aquinas, St. *Summa Contra Gentiles.* Translated by A. Pegis, J.F. Anderson, V.J. Bourke, and C.J. O'Neil. Notre Dame, Ind.: University of Notre Dame Press, 1975.

† Thomas Aquinas, St. *Summa Theologiae,* vol. I; *The Existence of God,* Part 1, Questions 1–13. Edited by Tho. Gilby. New York: Doubleday & Co., 1969.*

Thomas Aquinas, St. *Treatise on Happiness.* Englewood Cliffs, N.J.: Prentice-Hall, Inc., 1964.*

Eckhart, Meister. *Complete Works.* New York: Paulist Press, in press.

‡ Thomas à Kempis, *The Imitation of Christ.* Edited by F.W. Farrar. New York: E.P. Dutton & Co., 1976.*

John of the Cross, St. *Works.* Translated by K. Kavanaugh. Library of Christian Classics, 1973.

REFORMATION AND COUNTER-REFORMATION CLASSICS

Luther, Martin, *Lectures on Romans.* Edited by W. Pauck. Library of Christian Classics, vol. 15., 1961.

Luther, Martin, *Luther's Works.* Vol. 42, Devotional Writings, I. Edited by M.O. Dietrich; Vol. 43, Devotional Writings, II. Edited by G.K. Wiencke. Philadelphia: Fortress Press, 1969.

† Luther, Martin. *Selections From His Writings.* Edited by John Dillenberger. New York: Doubleday & Co., 1961.*

Luther, Martin. *Luther's Larger Catechism.* Translated by J.M. Lenker. Minneapolis: Augsburg Publishing House, 1967.*

† Erasmus, Desiderius, and Luther, Martin. *Discourse on Free Will.* Translated by F. Ernst. New York: Frederick Ungar Publishing Co., 1960.*

Zwingli, Ulrich. *Selected Writings.* Translated by S.M. Jackson. Philadelphia: University of Pennsylvania Press, 1972.*

† Calvin, John. *Institutes of the Christian Religion.* Edited by J.T. McNeill. Library of Christian Classics, vols. 20–21, 1960.

Calvin, John. *Theological Treatises.* Edited by J.K.S. Reid. Library of Christian Classics, vol. 22, 1954.

Williams, G.H., ed. *Spiritual and Anabaptist Writers.* Library of Christian Classics, vol. 25, 1957.

Simons, Meno. *Complete Writings.* Edited by J.C. Wenger. Scottsdale, Pa.: Herald Press, 1956.

Tappert, T.G., ed. *The Book of Concord.* Philadelphia: Fortress Press, 1959.

Council of Trent, 1545–63, Canons and Decrees. Translated by H.J. Schroeder. St. Louis: B. Herder Book Co., 1955.

Teresa of Avila, St. *The Way of Perfection.* Edited by E.A. Peers. New York: Doubleday & Co., 1973.*

‡ Ignatius de Loyola, St. *Spiritual Exercises.* Translated by A. Mottola. New York: Doubleday & Co., 1964.*

POST-REFORMATION CLASSICS

More, P.E., and Cross, F.L., eds. *Anglicanism.* London: SPCK, 1962.

‡ Hooker, Richard. *Of the Laws of Ecclesiastical Polity.* New York: E.P. Dutton & Co., 1954.

Wollebius, J.; Voetius, G.; Turretin, F. *Reformed Dogmatics.* Edited by J.W. Beardslee. Grand Rapids, Mich: Baker Book House, 1977.

Spener, Philipp J. *Pia Desideria.* Translated by T.G. Tappert. Philadelphia: Fortress Press, 1974.*

Bunyan, John. *Pilgrim's Progress.* New York: Penguin Books, 1965.*

Pascal, Blaise. *Pensees.* Translated by W.F. Trotter. New York: E.P. Dutton & Co., 1958.*

Law, William. *A Serious Call to a Devout and Holy Life.* New York: E.P. Dutton & Co., 1972.

Wesley, John. *Forty-Four Sermons.* Naperville, Ill.: Alec R. Allenson, 1944.

Wesley, John. *Journal, A Selection.* Edited by P.L. Parker. Chicago: Moody Press, 1974.*

† Edwards, Jonathan. *The Nature of True Virtue.* Ann Arbor, Mich: University of Michigan Press, 1960.*

Schleiermacher, Friedrich. *Brief Outline of the Study of Theology.* Translated by T.N. Tice. Atlanta, Ga.: John Knox Press, 1966.*

Schleiermacher, Friedrich. *The Christian Faith.* Edited by H.R. Mackintosh and J.S. Stewart. New York: Harper & Row, 1963.

† Schleiermacher, Friedrich. *On Religion: Speeches to Its Cultured Despisers.* Translated by John Oman. New York: Frederick Ungar Publishing Co., 1955.*

GENERAL ANTHOLOGIES OF SHORTER SELECTIONS

† Leith, John L., ed. *Creeds of the Churches.* Atlanta, Ga.: John Knox Press, 1973.*

† Bettenson, H., ed. *Documents of the Christian Church.* Oxford: Oxford University Press, 1970.*

Forell, George, ed. *Christian Social Teachings.* Minneapolis: Augsburg Publishing House, 1971.*

MULTI-VOLUME CRITICAL EDITIONS OF CLASSICAL CHRISTIAN TEXTS

Quasten, J., and Plump, J., ed. *Ancient Christian Writers,* 22 vols. New York: Paulist Press.

Roberts, A., and Donaldson, J., eds. *Ante-Nicene Fathers,* 10 vols.

Payne, Richard J., ed. *Classics of Western Spirituality.* New York: Paulist Press, in press.

Deferrari, R.J., ed. *The Fathers of the Church,* 66 vols. Gaithersburg, Md.: Consortium Books.

Baillie, J., McNeill, J.T., and Van Dusen, H.P., eds. *Library of Christian Classics.* 26 vols.

Dillenberger, John, ed. *A Library of Protestant Thought,* 13 vols. Oxford: Oxford University Press.

Page, T.E., et al., eds. *The Loeb Classical Library.* Cambridge, Mass.: Harvard University Press.

Schaff, Philip, ed. *Nicene and Post-Nicene Fathers of the Christian Church.* First Series, 14 vols.; Schaff, Philip and Henry Wace, eds. Second Series, 14 vols.